"Rich in historic and visual detail, *Women of the Dawn* gives a poignant and compelling voice to long silent Native American women. . . . The book evokes powerful and haunting emotions."—Jill E. Shibles, president, National American Indian Court Judges Association

"Penobscot women, like all Wabanaki women, have long been the guardians of their people. The four women profiled by McBride possessed energy and power that strengthened and sustained them. They changed the lives of those with whom they came in contact. A rare glimpse of these women can be seen within the pages of this book."—Donna M. Loring, Penobscot Nation tribal representative

"I was enthralled by the passion and perseverance of the four Women of the Dawn whose courageous spirits ensured the survival of tribal lifestyles and values."—Virginia Driving Hawk Sneve, author of *Completing the Circle*

"An excellent portrayal of four Native American women."—Hazel V. Jimerson Dean, Wolf Clan mother, Allegany Seneca Nation

Women of the Dawn

Bunny McBride

University of Nebraska Press

Lincoln and London

First Bison Books printing: 2001

Library of Congress Cataloging-in-Publication Data

McBride, Bunny. Women of the dawn /

Bunny McBride. p. cm. Includes bibliographical ref-

erences.

ISBN 978-0-8032-8277-3

1. Abenaki women – Biography. 2. Abenaki women –

History. 3. Abenaki women – Social life

and customs. 4. New England – Biography. I. Title.

E99.A13M43 1999 305.48′8973-dc21 99-20617 CIP

Dedicated to my American Indian women friends, who have taught me much about strength and resilience – especially

Dr. Eunice Bauman-Nelson

Dr. Hazel Jimerson John

Sarah Lund

Jean Archambaud Moore

Elizabeth Phillips

Mary Sanipass

CONTENTS

Acknowledgments ix

Introduction xi

PORTAGE 1

1. Moon of Ripening Berries:
Molly Mathilde (Marie Mathilde),
ca. 1665–1717 5

PORTAGE 39

2. Moon of Freezing Rivers:
Molly Ockett (Marie Agathe),
ca. 1740–1816 43

PORTAGE 69

3. Moon of Blinding Snow:
Molly Molasses (Mary Pelagie),
ca. 1775–1867 73

PORTAGE 95

4. Sowing Moon: Molly Dellis
(Mary Alice Nelson Archambaud),
1903–1977 99

PORTAGE 133

Methodology and References 135

Illustrations 152

ACKNOWLEDGMENTS

My greatest debt of gratitude is to my husband, Harald Prins. Without him this book would never have made it to the finish line. I thank him for the sharing of ethnographic knowledge, for being a hawk on historical details, and for doggedly reminding me of my goal to write the stories of these remarkable women in a way that would embrace a wide audience. I also thank him for his steadfast enthusiasm and encouragement, evidenced in his willingness to critique numerous drafts of the manuscript, but most of all I thank him for his love and loyal friendship.

I wish to express my appreciation to the following people who read the manuscript at various stages and offered valuable input: Susan Els, my sister, fellow writer, and dear friend; Jean Archambaud Moore, Molly Dellis's daughter and the most selfless informant I know; and Donna Loring, tribal representative to the Maine state legislature. I also wish to thank the scholars whose critical reviews of the manuscript fueled the writing of my final draft. Emerson Baker and an anonymous reviewer each drew attention to helpful references, Baker concerning Molly Mathilde and the other reviewer concerning Molly Ockett's childhood exile in Massachusetts. Colin Calloway's comments prompted me to better address the needs of more traditional "bread-and-butter" historians by identifying for the readers the reconstructed scenes in the book.

Finally, I wish to acknowledge the many American Indian women and men who helped provide the foundation and purpose essential to the writing of this book. Through the years they have shared their knowledge, stories, and hospitality with me, and in numerous cases their friendship.

INTRODUCTION

Women of the Dawn traces the lives of four Wabanaki Indian women. (*Wabanaki* means Dawnland, and it is the collective name given to Algonquian-speaking tribes living near the North Atlantic coast[1] – where the light of dawn first touches the American continent.) These women shared the same first name, Mary – bestowed by Catholic missionaries, but distinctively pronounced by Wabanakis as "Molly." Beyond a name, they shared a tragedy born of European contact. In the face of this tragedy, they all dared to bridge the gap between their own worlds and that of the European strangers who invaded their continent. Yet each woman possessed enough passion and perseverance to resist being swallowed up by the pervasive ways of the newcomers and to hold on to a vital core of herself and Wabanaki culture. As mothers, they bore seeds of continuity, rooted in the past, branching toward the future.

The book spans four centuries. It begins with Molly Mathilde, who was born on the eve of the Wabanakis' disintegration, and ends with Molly Dellis, born at the dawn of their regeneration. Because Molly Dellis actually researched Molly Mathilde's life, the stories form a circle, and Molly Dellis serves as narrator for each biography. Echoing the fact that all four women canoed the region's woodland rivers and moved from one stream to the next by way of foot-worn portage routes, the book carries readers from one profile to the next by way of brief "portages." The portages are vignettes of Molly Dellis at critical passages in her personal life, moments when she contemplates the experiences of her female forebears in search of insight. Gazing into the distant mirror of their lives, Molly Dellis comes to know these women and brings them forward into her own life. Holding them in thought, she faces herself and gathers strength to carry on. Their stories become her story.

Combined, these brief biographies tell the long saga of colonization in northeastern America from the rare vantage point of women.

---

1. Today's surviving Wabanaki communities include the Abenakis, Maliseet, Mi'kmaq, Passamaquoddy, and Penobscot.

They wed fact with feeling, and each story is a step in a spiritual pilgrimage from innocence to shrewdness to bitterness to wisdom. The journey is represented metaphorically by linking each life to a particular season – the bountiful ease of summer, the foreboding of fall, the destitution of winter, the promise of spring.

Beyond biography, history, and spiritual journey, *Women of the Dawn* is a challenge to stereotypical views of American Indian women; the individuals in this quartet are gloriously distinct from one another. At the same time, the shared aspects of their lives – especially motherhood and their struggle against colonialism – show the vital roles that Native women play in the cultural survival of tribes. Each woman, in her own way – and in her unique time and circumstances – faced the question, *What of the past will be carried into the future?* The answer to that question lies not in this book, but in the lives of all of us, Indian and non-Indian alike.

Readers interested in this book's theoretical orientation, research methodology, and writing strategy may refer to the Methodology and References section at the end of the book.

WOMEN OF THE DAWN

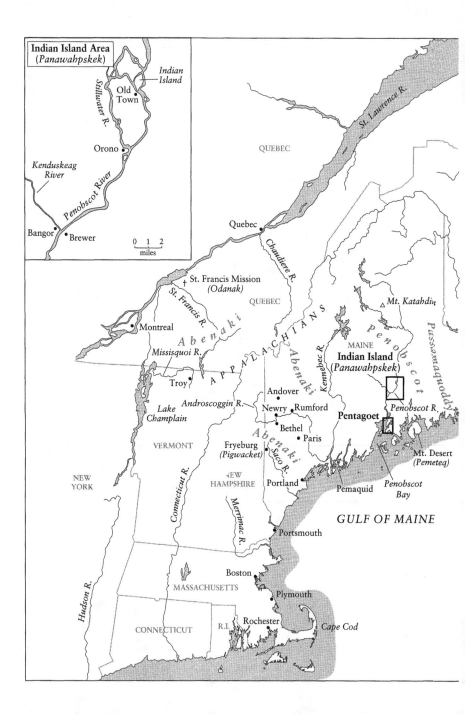

Indian Island Area
(Panawahpskek)

Indian
Island

Old
Town

Stillwater R.

Orono

*Kenduskeag
River*

Penobscot River

Bangor
Brewer

0 1 2
miles

QUEBEC

St. Lawrence R.

Quebec

Chaudiere R.

St. Francis Mission
(Odanak)

St. Francis R.

QUEBEC

Montreal

A b e n a k i

Missisquoi R.

Troy

A P P A L A C H I A N S

A b e n a k i

Kennebec R.

△ *Mt. Katahdin*

MAINE

Penobscot

Indian Island
(Panawahpskek)

Passamaquoddy

Andover

Androscoggin R.

Newry   Rumford

Pentagoet

Lake
Champlain

Bethel

Penobscot R.

VERMONT

Paris

NEW
YORK

A b e n a k i

Fryeburg
(Pigwacket)

Saco R.

Connecticut R.

NEW
HAMPSHIRE

Portland

Pemaquid

*Penobscot
Bay*

Mt. Desert
(Pemeteq)

GULF OF MAINE

Merrimac R.

Portsmouth

Hudson R.

Boston

MASSACHUSETTS

Plymouth

CONNECTICUT

R.I.   Rochester

Cape Cod

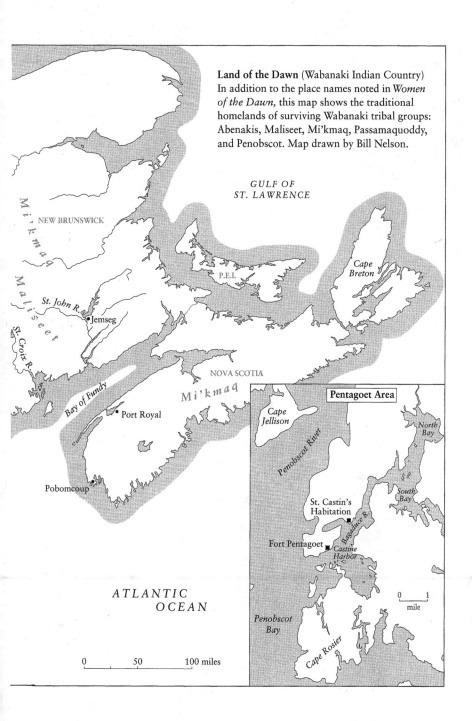

Land of the Dawn (Wabanaki Indian Country) In addition to the place names noted in *Women of the Dawn,* this map shows the traditional homelands of surviving Wabanaki tribal groups: Abenakis, Maliseet, Mi'kmaq, Passamaquoddy, and Penobscot. Map drawn by Bill Nelson.

GULF OF ST. LAWRENCE

NEW BRUNSWICK

Mi'kmaq

Maliseet

Cape Breton

P.E.I.

St. John R.

St. Croix R.

•Jemseg

NOVA SCOTIA

Mi'kmaq

Bay of Fundy

• Port Royal

Pobomcoup

Pentagoet Area

Cape Jellison

North Bay

Penobscot River

South Bay

St. Castin's Habitation

Fort Pentagoet

Bagaduce R.

Castine Harbor

ATLANTIC OCEAN

0   1
mile

Penobscot Bay

Cape Rosier

0   50   100 miles

PORTAGE

Long ago, Indians who lived in the Dawnland moved through vast forests on rivers that laced the land and linked its farthest reaches to the sea. In the winter they tied snowshoes on their feet and trudged the frozen waterways. During the rest of the year they traveled more easily in bark canoes, poling upstream or paddling downstream with the current. When a watercourse became dangerously difficult or diminished to a trickle, or when people wished to move from one river valley to another, they pulled their lightweight boats ashore and carried them over age-old portage paths through shadowy woodlands. Each portage spoke of challenge and change and new beginnings.

February 1935: Manhattan, New York City

On a late winter afternoon the sun slipped below the windows of the New York Public Library, and the main reading room fell into shadow. A petite, dark-eyed woman drew her coat around her shoulders and continued making notes in minuscule script. Her regal silhouette caught the attention of others in the room as they paused and absentmindedly glanced up from their books. One person after another felt their eyes wander in her direction. They gazed at her finely cut features and the elegant slant of her neck. They stared at the odd style of her raven-hued hair, parted in the middle and wound into two glossy coils, one over each ear. The bold ones scanned her figure, pausing when they reached the firm curve of her calves. Then, reacting to her disciplined posture, they straightened up a bit in their chairs and turned back to their work.

Molly Dellis Nelson had firm legs because she was a dancer – a Penobscot Indian dancer from Maine who had lived and performed in Europe. A year earlier she had left Paris to give birth to her child at

1

home. The Great Depression coupled with Europe's intense political turmoil kept her from going back across the Atlantic with her new daughter. But France remained in her thoughts. Seated at one of the public library's heavy oak tables, she pored over leather-bound books chronicling the seventeenth-century relations of Indians and Europeans. In particular, she hunted information about an Indian woman whose first name matched hers. Records referred to this woman by her Catholic baptismal name, Marie Mathilde, but her own people probably called her "Molly," the Native pronunciation of "Marie." Whatever she was called, this daughter of a great Penobscot River chief was an ancestral guide for Molly Dellis's worldly explorations, for Marie Mathilde had made a pioneering step across a vast cultural divide: she had married Jean Vincent d'Abbadie, the Baron of St. Castin.

The centuries-old story of Marie Mathilde and the French adventurer had quickened Molly's imagination since childhood. Now, however, it was an obsession, for she too had fallen in love with a Frenchman named Jean – Jean Archambaud, a *Paris Soir* journalist and the father of her child. Jean had sent her pages of notes about St. Castin, gathered in French archives and libraries, and now she aimed to flesh out Marie Mathilde's life to see how it fit with that of St. Castin. With an ocean between them, Jean and Molly hoped to coauthor a story about a love affair that foreshadowed and somehow fortified their own unorthodox union. More than this, Molly sought insight into bygone days that might help her mend the fractured traditions she had inherited. A journey into Marie Mathilde's life was a pilgrimage toward a time when Indian hearts were yet unbroken, a chance to piece together her own splintered soul.

A chime sounded, warning that the library would close in fifteen minutes. Molly sighed. It had been a long day, and she felt weary and restless. Putting down her pen, she closed her eyes and bowed her head so she could massage the back of her neck. Then, head still bowed, she dropped her hands to her lap and in the solitude of her thoughts tried once again to envision this seventeenth-century Penobscot Indian woman.

It was not easy to picture her, for in Marie Mathilde's day European explorers, traders, and officials took almost no note of women.

References about her in colonial documents and history books were made in passing, all in connection with her father and her husband. Novelists and poets, including the great Longfellow, had penned melodramatic phrases about her legendary beauty, but their verbal portraits captured little more than the Indian princess of popular imagination. Like tin mirrors, they revealed nothing of her soul. Molly knew better than to trust these delusive depictions, for she too had been chronicled by writers who savored idealized image over genuine substance. None saw beyond her stage name, Molly Spotted Elk, an icon of the romantic Indian, a commodity created for public consumption. At times their hollow words worked on her like demons, leaving her as empty as the icon itself. Her fear of this emptiness, as much as her love for Jean, drove her research. If she could truly *find* Marie Mathilde, if she could grasp and understand this foremother's ephemeral presence, perhaps she would achieve the fullness of her own being.

The final warning bell chimed. Molly stood, pulled on her winter coat and gathered up the paltry notes she had made that day. Given the scarcity of written information about Marie Mathilde, she could see only one way to reveal her soul. First, she would find the contours of this woman by painting around her, by marking out the natural and historical setting in which she had lived. Then she would step inside, inhabit the silhouette and give it form by building with insight on the few known facts of her life. With patience, Marie Mathilde's portrait would emerge. Somewhere beyond the veils of history and literature stood a real woman, one who had left an imprint on life etched from the challenges she had suffered and the choices she had made. What traces in the faces and characters of her Penobscot descendants came from her? What secrets did she know that were now buried? Had she, centuries ago, planted the seeds of Molly Dellis Nelson's yearnings?

As Molly stepped out into the icy dusk of the winter's evening, her thoughts remained so centered on Marie Mathilde's story that she barely noticed the cold.

CHAPTER ONE

Moon of Ripening Berries

Molly Mathilde (Marie Mathilde), ca. 1665–1717

*The Moon of Ripening Berries waned,
and its fruits fell to the ground or hung on
stems like drops of blood. Death seemed
to be everywhere. Yet, in the fruit
were seeds.*

WABANAKI PEOPLE WERE all well acquainted with her looks. Everyone recognized the flow of raven hair; the smooth, coppery skin; the oval eyes, dark as pitch; the high, curved brow and cheeks; and the wide, slender mouth and gleaming teeth. Not one of these features was unusual among her people, but no one could remember seeing all of them so gracefully arranged before they appeared in Molly Mathilde. It was as if the best parts of themselves had been summoned together into one exquisite whole. Because of this, Molly Mathilde seemed thoroughly unique, yet perfectly familiar.

Originally, her name was Pidianiske. She was born about 1665 in a forest of pine and birch on the banks of the great Penobscot River, which flows down from the mountains of Maine's heartland into the Atlantic Ocean. Like other tribes living near the northern Atlantic seaboard, Penobscot River inhabitants were called Wabanaki (People of the Dawn) by their inland neighbors, for each morning the first sunlight on the continent belonged to them. And they belonged to it, for they believed that Kisuhs, the great Sky Fire, was the ultimate spirit-power in a world in which everything was imbued with a sacred force.

During the summer, daylight came early, stayed late, and transformed the rugged region into a land of plenty. The season's bounty enabled scattered, individual families that had spent the miserly winter months inland to come together in large coastal encampments of a hundred or more people without fear of exhausting resources. Pidianiske's family often summered with others at the tip of a wooded peninsula embraced by the Penobscot and Bagaduce Rivers. From the shore the land rose gradually to a ridge that overlooked the vast mouth of the Penobscot and its scattered offshore islands to the southwest.

The Bagaduce, a more modest stream, curved around the peninsula's southeast flank to join the Penobscot as it poured into the ocean. Beyond the Bagaduce rolled spruce-covered hills, backed by the heroic silhouette of bare-granite peaks on Pemeteq (Mount Desert Island). Some days mist rolled in from the sea, weighting the air with a damp, salty scent and blotting out landmarks. Other days the air held a blueness so clear that it looked as if it might shatter – and so it did when shifting winds grabbed fistfuls of water and threw them against that crystalline sky.

While camped on the coast, Pidianiske's father and the other men fished, hunted seals, and searched the forests for giant white birch trees, the bark of which they used to make canoes that were light and swift. Her mother and the other women wove baskets and fashioned birch-bark containers. With their children they gathered fruits, roots, nuts, and shellfish, and prepared smoked fish and dried berries to be stored for the stark winter months. While working, they chewed spruce gum, which was used to caulk canoe seams – and which kept their teeth white and strong. Throughout the warm season, Penobscots did much socializing, celebrating the bond of their extended families and renewing friendships with people from allied clans. Each clan was named for an animal such as the bear, beaver, whale, or eel.

For young people the summer months at the coast offered romantic possibilities, not only with Penobscot River valley inhabitants from different clans, but also with members of various other Wabanaki tribes who were part of their wide social world. Pidianiske's parents, hailing from opposite sides of the Penobscot River, met during such a summer gathering. Her mother was an Abenaki from a chieftain family of the Kennebec River valley to the southwest. Her father was a Maliseet whose band roamed between the Penobscot and the St. John Rivers to the northeast. A tall and dignified leader, he was known for his bold and insightful decisions. As a young man he had risen to the position of chief in the Penobscot River valley. His marriage extended his personal ties to the Kennebec, and during Pidianiske's childhood he became the grand chief of Maine's entire coastal area.

Pidianiske learned to respond to nature's shifting moods as she and her relatives moved about seasonally to meet their basic needs.

Each autumn, when frost paled the meadows and fallen leaves formed bright skirts around the trees, most Wabanakis departed from the coastal lands. Paddling and portaging inland, they scattered into small family groups for the fall hunt. Men stalked prey and tended traplines. Women skinned the animals and transformed the furs and hides into clothes, moccasins, and blankets to shield their families from winter's icy breath. Winter was so stingy that Wabanakis called January the "Moon That Provides Little Food Grudgingly." Even as a child, Pidianiske realized that during this season her people had to rely on their own mettle rather than on nature's meager offerings. Temperatures plunged far below freezing, and game diminished due to animal patterns of hibernation and migration. Hunters, wearing snowshoes and working with small dogs, managed to chase down caribou and moose, cornering them in snowdrifts for the kill and hauling the quarry home on toboggans. Other sustenance came from bark-lined root cellars, which were stocked with provisions taken up in kinder seasons. When hunters failed to find game, they turned to shamans. Because shamans had *m'teoulin* (magic powers), they could see things others could not – the past, the future, enemies sailing beyond an offshore island, or game in a faraway valley. Shamans had many ways of calling up such visions. Sometimes they filled a great birch-bark dish with water, gazed into the liquid mirror, and went into a trance until the vision they were looking for appeared on the water's surface.

Throughout winter's reign Pidianiske's life centered on the hearth in her family's large birch-bark wigwam. Glowing embers filled the air with quivering light and heightened the sweet scent of the hemlock boughs that carpeted the ground. Sitting upon fur blankets, her mother nursed the youngest child and showed Pidianiske how to mend clothes and embroider them with dyed moose hair or porcupine quills. Her father, crouched on his heels by the fire, roasted chunks of meat or repaired his weapons. After nightfall, as Pidianiske and her siblings nodded off, the age-old murmur of singing or storytelling danced about the shelter. It mingled with smoke from the fire and tobacco pipes and drifted out into the frigid darkness through an opening in the peak of the wigwam. Even the harshest season had its pleasures.

Well into March, frozen waterways and deep snow hampered long-distance travel. Most Wabanakis remained inland until they received clear signs of winter's end. Before anyone explained those signs to Pidianiske, she knew them – *felt* them. First came the long, low groans of rivers and lakes as their frozen backs began to shrink and shift in the warming air. Then, as loud as thunderclaps and as swift as lightning, fractures bolted across each sheet of ice until it began to split into great slabs. Soon ice cakes floated atop open waters and out to sea. Their departure signaled the coming of spring and the arrival of Spear-Fish Moon, a time when families canoed to falls and rapids to spear and net salmon, smelt, and other spawning fish. As leaves unfurled and painted green upon the spaces between branches, Wabanakis rode the current downriver, camping along the way and gathering bird eggs and fiddlehead ferns. Then, once again, they arrived at the coast for the summer. There they stayed until the Moon of Ripening Berries waned to a mere sliver of light in the night sky.

Pidianiske's grandmother told her one particular story more often than any other. She always began the tale the same way – just as her own grandmother had told it to her: "Long ago, just after the geese had flown north, the Old Ones saw something odd on the horizon of the big water. At first, they thought it was a floating island or a great white bird, but soon they realized it was the fulfillment of an ancient foretelling – that bearded strangers would come to Wabanaki Country in great sailing boats from the direction of the rising Sky Fire."

In fact, it was the ship of Giovanni da Verrazano, an Italian navigator hired by the king of France in 1524 to find a passage to China. In the course of the century, a handful of other European explorers steered ships into Penobscot Bay and nosed around the river's mouth. Their brief encounters with Penobscot River folk were fraught with tension as well as mutual wonder, and they almost always included a bit of ceremonial barter. These early visits enlivened stories told around wigwam hearths, but otherwise life here continued as it had for more than a hundred thousand moons.

By the time of Pidianiske's grandmother's birth in the early 1600s, European merchants had figured out that large profits could be made from the fur-bearing animals that roamed Wabanaki forests. So they set up trading posts along the Atlantic seaboard. The peninsula inhabited by Pidianiske's people was enticing to the newcomers for its closeness to excellent fishing grounds, its fine stands of timber, and its inland streams and forests teeming with beaver, marten, and otter. In addition, it offered a protected anchorage accessible by waterways deep enough for large sailing ships. The natural resources of the region and the strategic location of the peninsula spelled competition. Both French and English merchants ventured there in the first decades of the century. Mispronouncing local Indian names for the area, the French called it Pentagoet, the English, Penobscot.

In 1629 English traders from the fledgling Pilgrim settlement at Plymouth Colony expanded their operations northward and built a fortified trading post on the peninsula, but they did not hold on to it for long. During the next hundred years this site would change hands several times, for it stood in a contested area of overlapping French and English colonial claims – at the southern end of the French colony of Acadia and at the northern end of a territory the English called the Province of Maine.

Although both foreign powers claimed the lands of the Wabanaki, colonial rivalry made it too dangerous for white farming families to settle in the Penobscot Bay area. Harsh winters and a short growing season discouraged them as well. So, throughout the 1600s the strangers used the point of land frequented by Pidianiske's people as little more than a trading outpost and military stronghold. Still, their impact on Indian life was momentous. Epidemics born of European contact periodically ravaged tribal villages up and down the coast. Sometimes these scourges left more people dead than alive. Pidianiske's grandmother had lost many loved ones to the mysterious diseases during her childhood. She had vivid memories of whole communities in mourning, their faces painted black with soot and bear grease. As an old woman, she told her granddaughter about these horrible losses, but she could not begin to explain the deep sorrow and confusion that she and other survivors felt in the face of such devastation. In time, Pidianiske would discover them for herself. Epidemics did much more than break the hearts of survivors. They ripped apart families; they broke up traditional trade networks and increased reliance on Europeans; they sorely tested age-old spiritual beliefs and made Wabanakis vulnerable to the influence of missionaries – and to alcohol.

So it was that the ancient roots of Wabanaki life had begun to fray when Pidianiske entered the world in 1665. The English had command of the fortified trading post at Penobscot Bay at the time and over much of Acadia as well, but the French soon reclaimed the post and the colony. The takeover came during the Moon of Ripening Berries in 1670 when Pidianiske was five years old. From her family's campsite among the evergreens she could hear the rolling drumbeats and booming cannon fire announcing the ceremonial changing of the guard. The thunderous sounds so filled her heart with both fear and wonder that she wanted to cower at home and at the same time to run to the scene of the turmoil. Finally, she and her siblings answered curiosity's call. Slipping away from camp, they scurried toward the fort and came within sight of it in time to witness the lowering of one flag and the raising of another. After two soldiers in red coats folded the fallen banner, they and their comrades marched shoreward in formation, boarded several longboats, and rowed out to the grand warship at anchor in the bay. Pidianiske watched as they hoisted white sails as big as clouds and glided out toward the deep blue horizon. As the ship faded in the distance, she turned her gaze back to the fort. A man dressed in blue was rallying his soldiers to haul in supplies and settle in to their new headquarters. Working among the troops was a young fellow who would soon change Pidianiske's life forever, just as she and her people would change his.

Jean Vincent d'Abbadie was born in 1652. He began life on a privileged note as the son of the first baron of St. Castin and his blue-blooded wife. A few months after his birth, Jean Vincent's mother died during a plague. In spite of this early loss the boy had a relatively carefree childhood. He and his father, along with his older brother and sister, lived in a small castle overlooking the Pyrenees Mountains, four hundred miles south of Paris. They were surrounded by a pastoral land dotted with vineyards and peopled with peasants, shepherds, and fishers. Jean Vincent's noble birthright entitled him to special hunting privileges in the region. It also provided the opportunity for an elite education and an officer's training position in the prestigious Carignan Regiment. In 1665, when Jean Vincent was just thirteen, King Louis XIV sent him and his regiment across the Atlantic to the French colony of Canada. They were given a charge that thrilled the boy soldier: that of subduing the fearsome Iroquois warriors whose relentless attacks threatened Crown holdings in the New World.

Along with the Carignan soldiers came regular troops. Sailing up the St. Lawrence River, they arrived at the colonial capital of Quebec with shiploads of supplies and horses, plus scores of French peasant families who planned to settle in the region. In the face of English rivals, the French Crown desperately needed colonists to secure its foothold in North America. More than fifty thousand English had put down roots in New England, while only nine thousand French had settled in Canada. The number of settlers was even more modest in the neighboring French colony of Acadia. That region, extending northeast from Penobscot Bay to Cape Breton and westward to the Appalachian Mountains, was home to fewer than four hundred French people – and about five thousand Wabanakis.

Within two years, Jean Vincent's regiment defeated the Iroquois and then disbanded. Officers willing to remain in New France received land grants and capital to start agricultural, fishing, or fur-trading businesses. Quite a few common soldiers became small-time fur traders. Roaming the woods from one Indian encampment to another, they spent most of their time beyond French settlements and became known as *coureurs de bois* (forest rovers). Some of the French rovers took Indian women as wives and became fathers of métis (mixed-blood) children. Unlike their Protestant neighbors in New England, the French had no policy of racial segregation.

About this time, Jean Vincent met Pidianiske's father, Madock-awando, who had come to Quebec for trade and diplomatic purposes. Intrigued by the chief and his tales, the young Frenchman ventured back to Penobscot Bay with him and decided that he would settle there after making a brief sojourn back to France. At home, Jean Vincent found news of his father's death awaiting him, along with a hard lesson about French inheritance customs. As second son, he received nothing from the family estate. The title of baron, and all the possessions that went with it, now belonged to his older brother.

This turn of events gave Jean Vincent all the more reason to seek his fortunes across the ocean.

So it was that on a sunstruck July day in 1670, Jean Vincent stood in the fort at Penobscot Bay, dressed in a handsome blue uniform. As the junior officer assigned to Acadia's newly appointed governor, Hector de Grandfontaine, the broad-shouldered youth took part in the ceremony in which the French formally reclaimed Fort Penta- goet from the English – while five-year-old Pidianiske watched from a distance.

Even in that moment of triumph, Jean Vincent understood that sooner or later the English would try to reclaim control over Fort Pentagoet, the gateway to Acadia. Countless skirmishes had already taken place in this region. Others were sure to follow as colonial powers fought for control over Indian resources, lands, and souls. The Wabanaki coast was not a place for the faint of heart, but it was a place for Jean Vincent d'Abbadie. Buoyed by an adventurous spirit and by the confidence of youth, Jean Vincent thought it a prize to guard a frontier outpost in a colony all but devoid of his countrymen and far from the controlling hands of French authorities in Quebec and Paris.

With his bold and independent nature, Jean Vincent felt more drawn to his Indian neighbors than to his fellow colonists. He built strong bonds with the Wabanaki, especially Pidianiske's father, Madockawando. These ties, along with a determination to speak the local language, helped him become a successful fur trader. In the spirit of a *coureur de bois* he left the fort often, roamed the woods, and spent many nights in wigwams. He shared freely with his Native friends, and as he did so his stature among them grew. As the son of the Baron of St. Castin, he had learned codes of honor, and he understood that a chief's status had as much to do with generosity of spirit as with courage. His position among Pidianiske's people was heightened all the more by the marksmanship skills he had gained through military training and growing up in a noble class with special hunting privileges. His greatest achievement in the eyes of Wabanakis, however, was the fact that he had fought their mortal enemy – the Iroquois – and emerged victorious.

Jean Vincent's prosperity, generosity, and military prowess, along with an intriguing blend of dignified manners and wilderness know-how, served him well when it came to what he admitted was his "weakness for women." As enterprising in love affairs as he was in trade, his many adventures with Wabanaki women soon earned him a questionable reputation in the French colonial community. His romantic exploits became the stuff of gossip – tasty tidbits that sometimes swelled to legendary proportions on the tongues of his countrymen. Word of his womanizing also spread among Indians, who turned stories of his sexual escapades into songs. On several occasions Pidianiske overheard Wabanaki women singing the bawdy tunes among themselves and laughing uproariously. Sometimes, when off on her own in the woods, Pidianiske chanted the ditties to herself. Not fully understanding the words but eager to claim for herself the raw joy of the women, she sang with gusto, now and then stomping her foot for emphasis.

Between Jean Vincent's dalliances, Pidianiske saw him quite often since her father was his most important contact in the Penobscot River valley. To reinforce his relationship with Madockawando, the Frenchman brought Pidianiske bright glass beads, ribbons as red as strawberries, and various other gifts sure to delight a young girl. She, also aiming to please her father, served Jean Vincent food when he came to their birch-bark home. Time and again she watched this foreigner and her father squat by her family's fire and rake out a coal to light the tobacco they smoked in long clay pipes imported across the big salt water. Her father, in turn, was a frequent guest within the formidable earthworks and stone walls of Fort Pentagoet. The fortress seemed oddly fixed to Madockawando, whose mobile lifeways made him favor the versatility of portable wigwams. The rough slate buildings that lined the fort's inner walls embraced a cobblestone courtyard. The buildings included a workshop, store-house, guardhouse, and soldiers' barracks, plus Commander Grand-fontaine's home and another smaller dwelling where Jean Vincent lived once he became second in command. Above the fort's entrance, bridging the gap between Jean Vincent's house and the guardhouse, stood a small Catholic chapel and belfry.

On occasion Pidianiske visited the chapel with her father, and it was there that she was baptized. With the ritual came a Christian name, and hers was Marie Mathilde – pronounced "Molly" Mathilde by Wabanakis. Pidianiske stumbled over the strange name and wondered how it rolled so easily off Jean Vincent's tongue. In time, she would master its sounds, and some of her own people would drop Pidianiske and call her Molly Mathilde, or simply Molly. To commemorate her baptism, Jean Vincent gave her a most appropriate gift: a silver cross to be worn as a pendant around her slender, brown neck. As she marveled at its shininess and fingered its smoothness, she did not yet understand that it had cost her her name and that it symbolized an agreement to change her spiritual identity and give up a part of herself. On the contrary, the ceremony made Pidianiske – *Molly Mathilde* – feel special, and obviously it pleased her father and his French companion.

Madockawando, like other Wabanaki leaders, viewed his daughter's baptism as a special ceremony that sealed a bond of friendship and obligation. While the curious ritual may have had some spiritual meaning to the chief, he also understood that those who participated in it gained stronger military ties with the French and easier access to firearms and other trade goods. He and his fellow tribesmen, however, did not deal exclusively with the French, for it was often easier and more profitable to trade with the English. Similarly, Jean Vincent's commander, Grandfontaine, found it necessary to permit and even participate in at least some commerce with the English in order to supply necessary goods for his garrison. After all, the French trading center at Quebec lay beyond the mountains, nearly three hundred miles away, and the waterways leading to it were frozen much of the year, while the nearest English trading settlement was just around the coastal corner at Pemaquid peninsula. Besides, English merchants paid more for furs, offered a wider array of goods, and frequently brought their business right to Pentagoet.

Ultimately, the French Crown called Grandfontaine to task for his commercial dealings with the English. Accused of selling furs to the enemy, he was pulled from Fort Pentagoet in 1673 and replaced by Jacques de Chambly, who had served as a captain in the Carignan Regiment. Chambly, also finding it impossible to finance the fort without doing business with the English, soon followed the same trading practices as had Grandfontaine. The consequences of his decision were dreadful. In the summer of 1674, an Englishman from Boston visited Pentagoet for several days under the guise of setting up business relations. Chambly welcomed the man and showed him about the place. A week later this visitor returned with a well-armed group of Dutch sea raiders and New England fishermen and attacked the fort. Outnumbering the French defenders three to one, the assailants severely wounded Chambly and forced most of his soldiers to swear allegiance to the Dutch Prince of Orange. When Jean Vincent refused to give oath, they tortured him. They burned the flesh between his fingers, holding fire to his hand until the skin turned black and began to ooze red. Then they pillaged and torched the fort.

During this onslaught Madockawando and his warriors had been seal hunting, and the attack may well have been timed to coincide with their absence. The Penobscot women and children had stayed behind, and the sound of violence shook the domestic calm of their camp. Pounding cannon fire collapsed the bastion's walls, and nine-year-old Molly Mathilde saw the sky darken as wooden beams and shingles went up in smoke. Drawn by the cries of mortally wounded men, she ran to the safe lookout atop the ridge. Crouched there, trembling, she watched the attackers force Chambly and Jean Vincent into a longboat. Even from afar she could tell that something was terribly wrong with Jean Vincent's hands. The heavy scent of spent gunpowder floated up to the ridge and hung in the air. Sniffing it, Molly Mathilde felt certain she would never see the dashing Frenchman again.

With two important captives and a bounty of loot in tow, the raiders rowed to their ship, boarded it, and sailed up the coast. After attacking and plundering every French settlement and outpost they could find, they rode the wind back to Massachusetts Bay. In Boston they sold their spoils and imprisoned Chambly. As soon as Jean Vincent had recovered sufficiently to travel, they sent him as an envoy to Quebec. He was to report the loss of Pentagoet to Canada's governor Frontenac and collect a ransom of one thousand beaver pelts for Chambly's release.

Jean Vincent made the difficult journey to Quebec by canoe and on foot, paddling and portaging through the vast forests of New England, snaking his way through passes in the Appalachian Mountains into the St. Lawrence River valley. By the time he reached Canada's capital, winter was in the air, so he was unable to return immediately to Boston to deliver payment for Chambly's freedom. Spending the cold months in Quebec, Jean Vincent came to know Governor Frontenac, who was impressed with his knowledge of the Wabanaki coast and its Native inhabitants. Recognizing the strategic value of Jean Vincent's unique relationship with the region's Indians, the governor charged him to go back to Penobscot Bay and secure local tribal support for the French cause. Since the French had lost military control over that region, Frontenac made the assignment in secret and instructed Jean Vincent to carry out his command in the guise of an independent agent. The order matched Jean Vincent's natural inclination, and it pleased him to realize that he was well on his way to fulfilling it.

Before leaving Quebec, Jean Vincent received the news that his older brother, who had succeeded their father as baron, had died. From such a distance, this death felt unreal to Jean Vincent. He had not witnessed the sorry event. He had not sat at his brother's bedside and held his hand, nor stood in holy silence as a priest gave the last rites. Instead, the dark news reached him many months afterward, written on a pale piece of paper neatly folded and secured with a wax seal. For Jean Vincent, the snap of that seal ended his brother's life and made him the third baron of St. Castin. Thinking about what it would be like to go home, he realized he did not feel drawn to France at all. He had lived nearly half of his twenty-four years abroad, and he felt strong ties to Acadia, especially to Molly Mathilde's people. Now that his father and brother were both dead, he felt even less connected to his homeland. With this in mind, he decided to postpone returning to France and follow through on plans to go back to the ruined fort at Penobscot Bay. He sent word to his older sister to handle the affairs of his ancestral estate with the help of her husband, a well-connected lawyer.

After Jean Vincent delivered the ransom for Chambly, the old commander returned to France. Meanwhile, the Dutch had made no effort to use Pentagoet as a strategic site, and the English ignored Penobscot

Bay for a time. They were too busy defending their settlements in southern New England against a bloody uprising by Wampanoags who were trying to push colonial intruders off their land. These circumstances provided an opportunity for Jean Vincent to return to Penobscot Bay and carry out Frontenac's order.

Molly Mathilde, like her father and other Wabanaki friends, marveled at seeing Jean Vincent alive, and they welcomed him back into their midst. His generosity made them all the happier to see him. He came bearing gifts, including something special for eleven-year-old Molly, and he came bearing his noble title, the Baron of St. Castin.

As it turned out, Frontenac's government was so focused on Canada that Jean Vincent, now known as St. Castin, received little official support for his secret assignment in Acadia. Nevertheless, ever resourceful and resilient, he thrived on his own and did much to defend this unprotected flank of France's colonial empire. Salvaging stones and timbers from Fort Pentagoet, he constructed a rustic home and storehouse just north of the ruins near a cove on the Bagaduce River. Having no troops and not wishing to live separately from the Indian community, he disregarded the usual fortress layout and erected no defensive works. Deftly, he rebuilt trade relations with the Wabanaki and eventually with the English as well. His home became a busy trading post and the center of a seasonal Indian village. Some summers as many as thirty-two wigwams stood near the young baron's dwelling.

While fulfilling Frontenac's charge, St. Castin grew ever more at home with his Wabanaki neighbors. Soon the concerns and customs of Molly Mathilde's people became his own. He became fluent in the Wabanaki language, joined the Wabanakis in seasonal wanderings, and even participated in their tribal council meetings, which were often held at his home. When Madockawando and other chieftains entered his house at night, they always found a fire blazing in the gaping stone hearth of the living room. Red-hot flames licked huge logs to ashes and cast dancing shadows about a room filled with objects that reflected the baron's life on the wilderness edge of the French Empire. Here visitors saw benches of unpeeled balsam scattered among silk-cushioned chairs and other French furnishings that had come by ship from his home. Gun racks, bookshelves, wine racks, and animal trophies lined the walls. A crucifix hung above an altar that held votive candles. A broad, wooden table shouldered a spread of local and imported foodstuffs, served in bark bowls and on ceramic plates. Madockawando and his fellow chieftains spent many evenings in this room of contrasts, puffing on long-stemmed pipes and talking politics and trade. Typically, they sat on the dull wood floor and, like the baron, appeared in motley outfits – moose-hide moccasins, soft leather breechclouts, imported woolen blankets, and various parts of French military uniforms.

The packs of beaver pelts, sealskins, and moose hides stacked up in St. Castin's store gave testimony to his burgeoning wealth and to the number of Indians who chose to do business with him. He kept his post well stocked with the goods Molly Mathilde's people wanted in exchange for their furs: needles, scissors, and cloth; steel axes and iron kettles; arms, powder, and shot; wine, brandy, and tobacco; and flour, peas, and biscuits. Dependence on the fur trade made ammunition a most important commodity among Wabanaki hunters. To meet this need, St. Castin set up a lead-shot manufacturing workshop alongside his storehouse.

This was the summer setting for Molly Mathilde's growing-up years: the river, the sea, the forest, and an encampment that was still quite traditional, except for its one very odd and very fixed dwelling. As Madockawando's daughter, Molly Mathilde was always welcome in St. Castin's home. In the young baron's eyes, she belonged to the Indian version of a noble family, even though in Wabanaki society a chief was no more than first among equals. When Molly Mathilde visited, he humored her curiosity about his possessions. More than once she sat at the table in one of his grand chairs and turned the pages of leather-bound books filled with mysterious black symbols and drawings of faraway peoples and places. She listened in wonder as he tried to explain the words and pictures. The first sweet raisins she had ever tasted came from his hand, just as the first French phrases she learned came from his lips. Molly Mathilde enjoyed being spoiled by this man, even though it made her the subject of jealous gossip among other girls who had no such escape from the many household burdens shouldered by women in Wabanaki society. She responded to the baron's kindnesses by bringing him gifts – bark containers brimming with berries and embroidered moccasins and leggings made with her mother's help.

In 1680, England once again formally recognized French political rights over Acadia. Port Royal on the Bay of Fundy became the government seat of the French colony, but St. Castin remained at Penobscot Bay. Molly Mathilde turned fifteen that year and St. Castin, twenty-eight. She was becoming a young woman, and he was reaching the end of his long season of pleasure seeking. Tales of his sexual escapades, exaggerated by jealous fur-trading rivals trying to defame him, were undermining his reputation among colonial administrators, not to mention among zealous priests who sometimes stayed at his home. While it was acceptable and quite common for a Frenchman to marry an Indian woman, some of St. Castin's countrymen condemned his unrestrained cavorting as scandalous and improper. Moreover, it appeared to them that the reckless baron was adapting to the Indian way of life rather than the other way around as they felt it should have been. After all, he joined Wabanakis in their seasonal wanderings, and this was the very essence of *sauvage*, the term used by the French for "wild" or "uncontrolled," as well as for "Indian." Worse still, St. Castin sold furs to the English enemy. His name began to appear frequently in the reports and correspondence of French officials who criticized his highly irregular life.

Perhaps it was St. Castin's concern about his status, along with Molly Mathilde's emerging maturity, that caused him to look at her with new eyes. He began to notice the way the firelight traced the angles of her face, how the silver cross nestled in the hollow of her graceful neck, how the bright-colored dresses he gave her no longer hung straight, and how delightful her voice sounded when she used the French phrases he had taught her through the years. Molly Mathilde noticed this change in the Frenchman's attitude, but that did not prepare her for her father's announcement that he wanted her to marry St. Castin.

Madockawando, now grand chief of the coastal area that stretched from the St. John River to the Kennebec, would not make pointless demands on his daughter. His request stemmed from an understanding that his people would need strong French support to survive

English aggression that threatened to overshadow their lives. In 1676 a series of raids and skirmishes, known as King Philip's War, had ended with the full subjugation of Indians in southern New England. Thousands had been killed and dozens of Indian villages destroyed. Many survivors had fled to Canada, where they found refuge in French missions. Others had escaped to various river valleys in Maine. Their horror stories had stirred fear and anger among Wabanakis. During the next two years, reacting to stunning losses and to a series of random provocations, Wabanaki warriors on the Saco and Kennebec Rivers just south of Penobscot Bay had raided English settlements in their area. At first, Madockawando had pressed for peace, even as his neighbors and relatives urged him to take up arms. But early in 1677, English troops had come to the Penobscot under the guise of delivering a ransom for prisoners taken by Kennebec tribesmen, only to stage a surprise attack. They had plundered the camp, killed two chieftains and a dozen other warriors, and taken captives, including Madockawando's sister. This, among other hostile deeds, had prompted the chief to support his neighbors in their battles against the English. He was aided by arms and ammunition supplied by his friend St. Castin.

In the deadly arena of colonial competition, a marriage between Madockawando's daughter and a French nobleman and military officer would provide an essential bit of insurance for the chief and his people. In turn, it would give St. Castin (and the French Crown) a firm link to the two major Indian groups in southern Acadia: the Abenaki via Molly Mathilde's mother and the Maliseet via her father. There could hardly be a better match politically. St. Castin also would have a beautiful wife to warm his bed during long winter nights – and to ward off the judgments of colonial administrators and priests.

Molly Mathilde balked at her father's request. She liked St. Castin, but he was strange. Sometimes he wore outlandish and impractical attire, including colored wigs and hard-soled boots with spurs. When dressed like this, he had an odd scent about him that made her nostrils twitch with a mixture of discomfort and intrigue. Moreover, unlike Wabanaki men, he had an unseemly abundance of hair on his face and arms and hands. It was one thing to visit this man and accept gifts from him but quite another to have him as her husband and father of her children.

She took her objections to her mother, but her mother, albeit in a less extreme way, also had wed outside of her circle, stepping beyond the bounds of her Abenaki people in the Kennebec River valley to marry a Maliseet from far away. Seeing the widened security that came to her people through her union with Madockawando, she had little sympathy for Molly Mathilde's protests. Yes, she told her daughter, the Frenchman was strange, but he was not a stranger. Had he not given her special gifts from the time she was a child? Had he not slept in their wigwam and brought many conveniences to their people? Even though he was different, he had fought their deadly enemy, the Iroquois. He was as fine a hunter as any Wabanaki, able to stand as still as a stump while taking aim at a bear or moose. While it was true that he sometimes dressed oddly, he often wore clothing just like Molly Mathilde's father, such as the leather leggings and moccasins that they had made for him. Would she prefer one of those arrogant English traders who always kept their distance, as if they were better than the Wabanaki? St. Castin had never done that. He talked easily with her people, using their words and laughing heartily at their jokes. He could even tell clever jokes and stories himself, and tell them well. More than this, he had joined her father and other men in the sweat lodge, which made him clean in body and spirit. Perhaps most important, he had ventured with them to their winter camp, and he knew something of fitting life to nature's rhythms.

Molly Mathilde married Jean Vincent de St. Castin according to the customs of her people, which required him to hunt for his prospective father-in-law for a year or to offer up lavish gifts. Madockawando chose the gifts: a new pistol, a special sword, a tomahawk, and many other valued things. The groom also hosted an extravagant wedding feast, featuring mounds of roasted meat, barrels of red wine, fine tobacco, and high-spirited singing, dancing, and storytelling. In 1684 the Catholic Church blessed their union in a wedding ceremony officiated by a "blackrobe" (Jesuit priest) at the baron's rustic home. For this momentous occasion, St. Castin provided his bride with a long silk dress and silk bonnet befitting a French baroness. He himself donned a nobleman's outfit, including wig, ruffled white shirt, long brocade jacket, and high leather boots. Even at frontier outposts such as Pentagoet, French officers wore such apparel on important occasions. Daily attire for both St. Castin and Molly Mathilde was more practical and included varied ensembles reflecting both French and Indian fashion. Their wardrobes included white moose-skin robes and sealskin moccasins – some embroidered with French beads, others with shell beads or dyed porcupine quills. During the winter months they wrapped themselves in thick beaver or otter robes, and year-round each wore a silver crucifix. Madockawando, like other important allied chiefs, owned a French officer's coat, which he wore for special events, including his daughter's wedding to the Frenchman he had long called *nedabe* (my friend).

Romance may not have been the inspiration behind Molly Mathilde's marriage to St. Castin, but the mutual cares of a shared life gradually inspired love. Her husband's oddities became familiar and even endearing to her, and his kindnesses toward her grew more particular with each passing moon. Among the French, people commented that the baron had surrendered his former habits and that he often spoke of his commitment to his wife. Some said he changed for religious reasons or for political opportunism. But Molly Mathilde knew her husband was driven less by the rudders of his religion or politics than by the sails of his heart. She knew this by the touch of his hand and by the way his hazel eyes sometimes followed her as she moved about the room.

The next few years passed quite peacefully for the young Indian baroness and her French husband. Working closely with his father-in-law, St. Castin managed to steer clear of trouble in the dangerous borderlands. In 1684 Molly Mathilde gave birth to their first child, Bernard Anselm, followed by Thérèse in 1687, Joseph about 1690, and Marie Anastasie and Jean Pierre in 1692. Mixed-blood children were not unusual in New France, but they were rare in the Penobscot River valley, where very few non-Indians had ever made their home. Molly Mathilde's eldest son might well have been the first métis child she had ever seen, and his unique little face reflected the world of contrasts in which he would be raised.

In their early years Molly Mathilde's children spent little time with Europeans other than their father. From their mother and her relatives they gleaned the seasonal pulse of Wabanaki life and the survival skills needed to live in the wilderness. The forest, streams, and shores that surrounded them served as their playgrounds and training fields. They visited their grandfather Madockawando in his wigwam, as well as other Wabanakis who set up camp in the area. When tribal elders or representatives of far-away tribes met in their parents' home, these youngsters eavesdropped while the men smoked their pipes and discussed important matters in their native tongue. So Molly Mathilde's offspring were well acquainted with the landscape and language of their mother's traditions. In time they also experienced life beyond the forest and the wigwam. St. Castin owned a fast, flat-bottomed, twenty-two-ton sailing vessel. On occasion the children were invited aboard and sailed with their parents to Acadia's governmental headquarters at Port Royal, where St. Castin stored some of his goods for trade. Here, their father would conduct business and meet with colonial officials. Also, he and Molly Mathilde would make their confessions to the priest and purchase goods such as peas, flour, raisins, molasses, honey, spices, tobacco, and wine. The children marveled at the sights of the small French town. The great fort, built atop a hill, loomed large and cast a protective shadow over the governor's residence, guardhouse and barracks, chapel and cemetery, storehouses and mill. Sprawled over the landscape beyond the fort were frame houses, livestock pens, and a patchwork of orchards and vegetable gardens. Walking about the settlement, Molly's children encountered other métis youngsters, some of whom, like them, were destined to attend French colonial schools.

Among French officials, the blessing of St. Castin's marriage by the church, coupled with his ever-growing power, helped counter false rumors that he had a secret alliance with the English. While officials may have doubted such reports, they still weighed carefully the fact that the baron's influence among Indians could cause New France considerable damage if used against them. So they kept an eye on him and regularly assessed his reliability. In an official report written in 1687, Canada's governor noted, "St. Castin has been addicted in the past to libertinism, but he has very much reformed and has very good sentiments" toward the French Crown.

These good sentiments grew in 1688, when New England's new governor, Sir Edmond Andros, ransacked St. Castin's home and trading post. For a year Andros had tried to extend his power over the baron and over other French settlers living between the Penobscot and St. Croix Rivers. He had promised St. Castin rewards for allegiance to the English Crown, and he had showered Wabanaki leaders, including Molly Mathilde's father, with gifts in an effort to win them away from the French. When these efforts failed, he tried to intimidate St. Castin into submission by having his trade goods confiscated. Finally, in 1688 Andros set sail for Pentagoet in his swift warship, intending to confront the baron face to face. Hearing of his approach, St. Castin and Molly Mathilde shut up their home and store and retreated into the woods with their children. When Andros found the baron gone, he had his men ransack the place and haul off many precious goods. Before sailing back to the English fort at Pemaquid, he delivered another batch of gifts to Madockawando, telling the grand chief to inform his stubborn son-in-law that he could retrieve his belongings from Pemaquid when ready to pledge submission to the English Crown. Andros's audacity outraged Molly Mathilde. Not only were the French and English officially at peace at the time of the raid, but her father had signed a peace treaty with the English ten years earlier.

Andros's bold move cost the English many lives. When the colonial powers went to war again the next year, St. Castin rallied his Wabanaki allies to back the French cause with a vengeance. Even Madock-awando, who still leaned toward keeping peace with the English, sometimes joined the other war chiefs in leading raids against English strongholds and frontier villages. Beyond rousing Indian support, St. Castin sometimes personally coordinated the military action and prisoner exchange. Fearing St. Castin's great influence among Indians and his ability to provide them with arms, English officials persisted in pressing him to defect. At one point they offered to grant him a vast tract of land in the Penobscot River valley if he agreed to become an English subject. Hearing this, Molly Mathilde laughed bitterly: "What right do Englishmen have to offer our lands!" When her husband continued to resist their overtures, the English tried to kidnap him. To her great relief, that effort also failed.

Nonetheless, the enemy gained ground. In 1690 they seized Port Royal and destroyed Wabanaki villages on the Saco, Kennebec, and Androscoggin Rivers south of Penobscot valley. Even worse, they terrorized Indian communities by setting prices on all Indian scalps, be they men, women, or children. To Molly Mathilde, the English practice of scalping for bounty was horrifying and inhuman – a world apart from the Wabanaki custom of scalping enemy warriors as proof of courage in battle. It transformed people into merchandise – as if their scalps were beaver skins. Most appalling of all, it turned even the most innocent into prey. The possibility of her children being scalped so haunted Molly Mathilde that at times she awoke in the night with a start and darted to their beds to make sure they were safe. Kneeling beside them, she stroked their long, dark hair, taking comfort in the gentle breathing of their sound sleep.

On the heels of these aggressions the English built a massive stone fort on the coast at Pemaquid, halfway between the Kennebec and Penobscot Rivers. Molly Mathilde overheard her husband describe the fort to her father. Armed with twenty cannons and well-manned with troops, it was the most formidable stronghold on the Atlantic seaboard. Listening soberly to this news, Madockawando reasoned that because the ratio of English military to French had shifted so dramatically, continued warfare would be suicidal for his people. In 1693, anticipating English supremacy on the Wabanaki coast, he once again accepted peace overtures from the English and encouraged neutrality among his people. This placed Molly Mathilde in a delicate position. Although her husband had supported her father in some of his earlier peacekeeping efforts, he could hardly do so as a French military officer in the middle of a war unless he were willing to face high treason and its penalty of death. He stood firmly with the French. Since warfare was the domain of men, Molly Mathilde had no say in the matter. Even if she had, it would have been all but impossible to figure out which course was best for her people.

Most Wabanaki chiefs disagreed with Madockawando's strategy. They pressed him relentlessly until at last he agreed to join arms with the French against the English. Their alliance led to the capture of the Pemaquid fortress, viewed as invincible by just about everyone. This stunning victory, masterminded by St. Castin, began with a great ceremonial feast outside his and Molly Mathilde's Pentagoet home. It ended as soon as the English commander at Fort Pemaquid realized his garrison was hopelessly surrounded on all sides by two well-armed French warships and a battalion of soldiers and 250 Indians. After surrendering, the English were given safe passage to Boston, without their weapons. French soldiers hauled the fort's artillery onto their ships, and Wabanaki warriors claimed the English muskets. Then St. Castin and his men destroyed the enemy stronghold.

In 1698, after several more attacks and counterattacks, French and English officials ended the decade-long war by signing a treaty that once again left Acadia in French hands. Tribal representatives from the region also signed a peace treaty with the English. But the aftermath of this second colonial war was no more than a lull between storms – and during that brief but deceptive peacetime, Molly Mathilde's father died. Madockawando had forged protective alliances and survived many battles only to be felled by the invisible killer that had ended the lives of so many Wabanakis – a foreign disease. Given his political stature, French and English officials made written note of his passing. In contrast, the death of Molly Mathilde's mother – like that of most Wabanakis – went unrecorded, except in the hearts of her people.

Whenever warfare threatened life at Penobscot Bay, Molly Mathilde and her children retreated thirty-five miles inland to an ancient Wabanaki campground on an island in the Penobscot River. Wabanakis called the place Panawahpskek (Where the Rocks Spread Out), for it lay where the river's flow widened, just above the rocky ledges of a great waterfall. The island had been used seasonally for thousands of years, and its nearness to the coast and location above the falls now made it an ideal refuge. More than this, it lay near Katahdin, the Wabanakis' greatest and most sacred mountain. To see Katahdin's peak glow pink as it caught the first light of dawn was to know where one stood. In Molly Mathilde's day the island emerged as the central village for Penobscot River Indians, and in time it became known as Indian Island.

In the haven of this island Molly Mathilde's children explored the woods, caught fish in the shallow stream that sliced through the land, or paddled along the shore in their father's canoe to search for muskrat houses. Usually, muskrats built homes that looked like small beaver lodges, but sometimes they simply burrowed into the bank and built dens. Either way, they had several chambers and entrances, plus feeding platforms where they brought their banquets of plants, clams, frogs, and fish. Molly Mathilde told her youngsters to watch these furry friends closely, for humans could learn many things from muskrats: the importance of avoiding strong currents and rocky areas; how to use a canoe paddle as a rudder in the same way the animal swims by steering with its tail; and, most of all, the wisdom of having more than one escape route as a protection against sudden attack.

Sometimes the children pulled the canoe onto the sloping shore at the island's northeast end. There, in season, they picked wild strawberries, plopping the juicy fruit into their bark pails – and into their mouths. As their hands became scarlet and sticky, the oldest boy, Bernard Anselm, would tell how the English once tortured their father with fire. Holding his stained hand out in front of him, he would say, "Long ago, before our father married our mother, the English burned his hands until the skin was *this* red!" The story always ended with praise for their father's bravery.

During this time Indian Island also became a retreat for a French missionary priest named Pierre Thury. Frustrated by colonial conflicts near the coast, as well as by coastal fishers and traders who sold alcohol to his Indian flock, Father Thury sought a more remote site for his mission work. The island seemed ideal, offering a safe retreat from the perils of war plus isolation from European rabble-rousers. So, after securing official permission to settle there and build a chapel, the priest moved in.

Surveying his new fold, Father Thury saw special religious promise in Molly Mathilde's children and pressed her husband to send the youngsters to a Catholic school in Quebec. To St. Castin this seemed reasonable. He had left the comforts of his own family home at an early age. His experiences as a boy soldier had been tough, but they had prepared him well for the challenges he would eventually face. Now his children needed preparation. The old Wabanaki world was falling out from under them, and unless they learned to fly, they might plummet into some dark abyss. Going to school in Quebec would give them wings. Although Molly Mathilde understood this, she did not like the idea of sending her children so far from home to be placed in the hands of people she did not know. She had never ventured to this fortified colonial city – the place where her father had first met her husband – but St. Castin had described it to her. She knew that the fort, perched dramatically atop a cliff, overlooked the St. Lawrence River, a waterway even greater than the Penobscot. Nearby stood Governor Frontenac's stately residence, the school, a spired cathedral, and the chapels of various priestly orders, as well as a towering windmill, wheat fields, and a street lined with thick-walled, multistoried houses made of stone, with slate or cedar shingle roofs. At the foot of the cliff, near the port, stood the warehouses and grand homes of the chief merchants. Shops and taverns flanked narrow, winding streets. During the summer months, when twenty or thirty vessels anchored in the bay, sailors swarmed the taverns. Their raucous doings transformed the city into a place that stirred the imaginations of schoolchildren who were weary of Latin and religious study.

Clearly, Quebec was a world apart – a place where bodies of water met bodies of thought, sometimes colliding and creating great waves. Young people, even adults, could be swept away in that city and never find their way home. This frightened Molly Mathilde, but she did not resist the wishes of her husband and the priest. With sorrow in her heart, she let her children go, one by one. The oldest, Bernard Anselm, was the first to leave. As she watched him sail away, she sensed she was losing something of herself; certainly, she was surrendering the last small hold she had over the course of his life. It did not escape her that the rhythms of her children's days differed vastly from those of her ancestors and even of her own girlhood. In their short lifetimes, it often seemed that family migrations and decisions had more to do with reacting to the sudden violence of strangers than with responding to nature's predictable seasons or fundamental human needs. Her young ones had never experienced utter calm; even periods of relative peace were only pauses between battles. Through marriage Molly Mathilde had chosen sides and thus gained some security for herself and her people. But she had lost the freedom and certainty of traditional Indian life, and at the end of the day she slept less serenely than her forebears. Had her father's counsel been wrong? Should they have abandoned their coastal homelands, retreated deeper inland, and avoided the newcomers altogether? Such were the thoughts of a mother unable to imagine the future of her children.

As it turned out, one of them had no future. In 1701 Molly's youngest son, Jean Pierre, left for school in Canada just as his older siblings had done before him. Only nine years old when he arrived in Quebec, he spoke almost no French, and he barely had time to learn the language, for within a year he became ill and died. To lose a child in her arms would have been difficult, but to have her son die in the care of strangers in a far-away place was almost unbearable. On hearing of his death, Molly Mathilde fled into the woods. She ran blindly and without pause until the pounding of her heart filled the forest. Exhausted, she sat down among the pines and began to trace back in her mind the brief life of her boy. Coming to that time when she had carried him safely within her body, she wept.

As afternoon shadows merged into night, Molly Mathilde built a fire. In time, she pulled a burning stick from the blaze and snuffed its flame in a bed of sweet fern. She stroked the charred stick with her palm and smeared her face black with soot. Then, folding her hands and closing her eyes, she prayed for her child's soul. Midway through her prayer, she shivered. *Where is he?* she wondered. Had he joined the spirit world of her Wabanaki parents or was he in a Christian heaven? With unspeakable dismay, she realized she did not know.

During the decade of the second colonial war, St. Castin had ceased trading with the English, but the formal peace agreement of 1698, coupled with the scarcity of French trading possibilities on the frontier, prompted him once again to take up business with his New England neighbors. Without selling his furs to these foreign merchants he could not meet the needs of his community – ammunition for hunting plus staples such as biscuits, tobacco, peas, cloth, and thread. Molly Mathilde well understood that her father's death had greatly increased her husband's responsibilities toward her people, but French officials viewed things differently, especially after St. Castin's great supporter, Governor Frontenac, died. Uneasy as ever about their grip on colonial Acadia, the French fretted over the renewed relationship between the English and St. Castin's Wabanaki companions. In 1701 their worry turned to anger when they learned that tribespeople living in the crucial buffer zone between the Penobscot and Kennebec Rivers had met with the English to accept gifts and make peace yet again. Furious that St. Castin had not stopped his Indian friends, French officials formally condemned him for dealing with the enemy. To answer these charges of treason, the baron sailed to Port Royal to see Acadia's governor, who urged him to return to France and give a full account of his actions at the royal court in Versailles.

St. Castin had no choice but to follow the governor's advice. If he was to clear his name, he had to sail to France and plead his case. While he was there, he could also settle the affairs of his inheritance, which included numerous valuable holdings in addition to his title and the baronial estate at St. Castin. Given the festering turmoil in Acadia, he thought it wise to safeguard his aristocratic position and possessions across the ocean as a possible refuge for himself and his family. This done, he would sail back to Molly Mathilde and the children in the colony that had become his home. Before leaving for France he made arrangements to set up a fishing enterprise and build a new house on the lower St. John River when he returned to Acadia. There, beyond the shadow of New England, the lives of his loved ones might be less endangered. Such a move would require Molly Mathilde, now thirty-six, to leave the land most familiar to her, but her own father had long hunted in the St. John valley, and in his final years tribespeople there had recognized him as a chieftain. Occasionally, she had even gone there with Madockawando, so it was not alien territory to her. The more Molly Mathilde thought about the idea, the more it appealed to her. Maybe her four surviving children, now ranging in age from nine to seventeen, would finally live in peace.

When Molly Mathilde bade her husband farewell, she trusted he would return safely. After all, he had lived through greater challenges than a journey across the great salt water. He had fought the Iroquois, endured torture, and survived battles against the English. Moreover, her own brother had once traveled to France, and he had come home unharmed. Yet there was something unsettling about St. Castin's departure. In their farewells Molly Mathilde had never waved him cross the ocean, only to distant corners of her own homeland. How odd to scan the vast sea and try to picture him so far beyond the horizon. Although he had often told her about his homeland – its snow-peaked mountains and rich vineyards, as well as its large cities, grand palaces, and formal gardens – she could not really grasp what that world was like. Who wrestled more with this parting – the man who was returning to his birthplace as a stranger or the woman who could not begin to imagine her husband's destination?

The voyage across the Atlantic took about a month. What changes had occurred in France since Jean Vincent's departure as a boy soldier nearly four decades earlier! The palace at Versailles, barely more than a royal fantasy at the time, had become the centerpiece of an imposing complex of government buildings, mansions, and stables, with a sweeping threshold of gardens featuring heroic statues, shimmering pools, and grand fountains. There, at King Louis XIV's court, the baron answered accusations of inappropriate trade with the English. To his relief, Crown officials found his defense credible. Moreover, they recognized the fifty-year-old veteran as a key asset in the king's ambitious colonial aspirations. Here was a seasoned man of extraordinary experience. Keen-witted in strategic matters, he had invaluable personal contacts with Indians and an unrivaled reputation as a frontier guerrilla leader. The Crown was as anxious as he was for him to return to Acadia, but first, he had family matters that needed his attention.

Having redeemed his reputation, Jean Vincent de St. Castin traveled on horseback to his ancestral home, four hundred miles south of Versailles. Following a well-used pilgrimage route, he moved at a comfortable pace, reacquainting himself with the land and spending nights at roadside inns. With each passing day, the terrain grew more dramatic until he found himself in the foothills of the Pyrenees Mountains. At last he was home. But no warm welcome awaited him. During his absence, his older sister, Marie, and her husband, Jean de Labaig, had appropriated the family estate and come to view all of his possessions as their own. Picturing his perilous life as a frontier soldier and fur trader in a savage land an ocean away, they had never expected him to come home alive. Marie had even agreed to have the family's illustrious coat of arms registered in her husband's name. The sight of her youngest brother on her doorstep gave her no pleasure. As legitimate heir to the family's noble position and fortune, he posed a formidable threat to her reputation and purse. No one rankled at this more than Labaig. Having assumed power-of-attorney over the estate after the death of Jean Vincent's brother, he had no intention of giving it up to a late-coming heir who had suddenly stepped out of the wilds of North America.

Based in the beautiful city of Pau, St. Castin presented his case to the regional parliament there. Labaig, a shrewd and well-connected opponent, deftly created one legal obstacle after another, miring St. Castin in litigation. The case dragged on for months, until months turned into years. Finally, King Louis XIV, aiming to have St. Castin back in Acadia where he was essential to the French cause, demanded a quick judgment on the matter. But Labaig's cunning was so great that he managed to foil even a king's orders, and St. Castin, despite royal pressure, refused to return to Acadia before winning his full inheritance for the sake of his children. To hold his ground, yet appease the king, he offered to provide the Crown with a strategic plan for holding on to the colony.

Whenever the hapless baron sent word to Molly Mathilde, the letter took months to arrive; sometimes it never reached her at all. Unable to fathom her husband's predicament or the vast distance that separated them, her emotions swung wildly from lonesomeness to profound worry to a gnawing sense of possible betrayal and abandonment. Seeking relief, she often walked to a point where she could see the ocean. There, watching the outgoing tide, she told herself that departures foreshadowed returns.

By 1704 Molly Mathilde and the children were in the thick of yet another colonial war. It had started in the summer of 1703. Tormented by losses, Wabanaki refugees in Canada and the Penobscot valley had returned to their homelands in river valleys south of Acadia with one thing on their minds – vengeance. Attacking New England settlements, they had killed English farmers, mothers, and children, or taken them captive. In turn, the English had wreaked havoc on the Wabanaki as well as on French ports and settlements throughout Acadia. Once more they had plundered the region, and this time they had ransacked St. Castin's home. Worse, they had seized many hostages, including the baron's daughter who was being held in Boston for ransom. When this terrible news finally reached St. Castin in southern France, he raged over his inability to rescue his daughter, comfort his wife, and avenge the wrongs done to his family and friends. To him, their suffering loomed all the larger in light of the pettiness of his own predicament – a seemingly invincible quagmire of legal complications and bureaucratic bondage born of his brother-in-law's guile and greed.

St. Castin's anguish ended in 1707. Early that year, just after finally settling his estate, the fifty-five-year-old baron died. It was bitter irony that this free spirit who improvised and flourished in the wilds of Acadia was done in by lawyers and paperwork.

Some time passed before the woeful news reached Molly Mathilde. It came in a missive delivered by Bernard Anselm. Even a loving son could not soften such tragic news or quiet the fear and confusion it wrought. Six years earlier Molly Mathilde had bid her husband good-bye, trusting his promise that he would return. Now she faced a separation that knew no bounds. It was a terrible and disorienting blow. Not only had she lost the remarkable man she had grown to love, but also the security that his presence had given her people. Life had long been uncertain for her, but she had taken solace in knowing that her husband put their family before king, country, or personal gain. Who else among the French could she truly trust to protect the well-being of all she held dear? She could think of no one. At age forty-two she felt less sure than ever before – adrift in the gray waters of open sea with no reference point.

The year Molly Mathilde became a widow, three of her four surviving children married into elite French-colonial families. At Port Royal, just after the Moon of Ripening Berries, twenty-three-year-old Bernard Anselm exchanged vows with Charlotte d'Amours, whose father owned a large estate at Jemseg on the lower St. John River. Father Gaulin, a Catholic priest familiar with French settlers as well as Wabanakis, performed the ceremony. Two months later Molly's two daughters had a joint wedding, and once again Father Gaulin carried out the sacred rituals. The girls married men who were cousins to each other – grandsons of the famous Claude de la Tour, a pioneering French entrepreneur and early military commander in Acadia. Thérèse, twenty, married Phillip Mius, lord of Pobomcoup, an estate on the southern coast of Nova Scotia. Anastasia, just fifteen, wed Alexandre le Borgne, lord of Port Royal.

Picking up his father's mantle, Bernard Anselm maintained the trading post at Pentagoet and served with courage as a frontier guerrilla commander. Ranging between Port Royal and the St. John and Kennebec Rivers, he kept close ties with both his mother's and his father's people, always seeking a balance between the well-being of the Wabanaki and that of New France. Like his father, he was a born diplomat and he usually dressed in Indian clothing, even though an elegant uniform came with his position as a French officer. Among the Wabanakis and French alike, he gained a reputation as a humane and generous man with foresight and good sense.

During the troubled years after her husband's death, Molly Mathilde made her home at Pentagoet with Bernard Anselm, his French Acadian wife Charlotte, and the couple's young daughters. Following a now-established pattern, whenever violence threatened, the women and children took shelter upriver at Panawahpskek, the tribe's island village. When Molly Mathilde looked at her oldest son, she saw her father and her husband, for he had Madockawando's strong nose and dark hair and Jean Vincent's full mouth and hazel eyes. In character, too, Bernard Anselm resembled both men, and Molly Mathilde took comfort in the similarities. Whenever her son was away on military duty, she prayed that he would achieve the lasting peace that had proved so elusive even to men as formidable as Madockawando and St. Castin. Her prayers, no longer frantic, had become quiet petitions, simple yearnings of the heart that rarely came out in words. Often she sat by the river, sensing that the stream itself was a prayer, for its flow offered hope to a woman feeling bound. Each time Bernard Anselm returned home and told Molly Mathilde of the latest military skirmish or the death of a kinsman, he marveled at the calmness of her response. Somehow, daily life continued in the middle of sorrows heaped up one upon the other.

Despite his mother's prayers and his own impressive military and diplomatic skills, Bernard Anselm and his French soldiers and Indian allies could not hold the enemy at bay. In 1713 the French Crown officially surrendered nearly all of Acadia to the English. Soon thereafter, Bernard Anselm decided to cross the Atlantic to claim the inheritance that his father had worked so hard to secure. Molly Mathilde worried that he too would get caught in the sort of legal quagmire that had robbed her of her husband. She knew Bernard Anselm had received notice that the family estate and title had been denied to him on the grounds that he was an illegitimate child. This excuse bit into her soul far more deeply than the loss of property, for it invalidated her marriage and bastardized her son. She could hardly stop Bernard Anselm from going abroad to contest such insults. He went well prepared, armed with missionary certificates and other evidences of the legality of his birth. Once in France, he proved his case with surprising swiftness. Soon thereafter, he brought Charlotte and their daughters to Pau to live, and in 1717 Molly Mathilde's firstborn son took his rightful seat in the Parliament of Navarre, as a member of the region's landed nobility – as the fourth Baron of St. Castin. Sadly, Bernard Anselm did not long hold the cherished title, for he died in 1721, but his first daughter – Molly Mathilde's first granddaughter – inherited his title and estate.

No one knows what happened to Molly Mathilde after Bernard Anselm left Acadia. In all likelihood, she stayed at Panawahpskek in the company of her daughter Anastasia, who lived on the island with her husband and their children. Molly Mathilde's younger son, Joseph, followed in the footsteps of his father and brother. Gaining notoriety both as a French military officer and a Wabanaki chief, he struggled to retain the rights of Wabanakis in their homeland and to help the French hold on to the remnants of their lost colony.

Just as there is little record of Molly Mathilde's life, there is no record of her death. By the close of the eighteenth century, the footprints of her offspring had also vanished in the mist of time. Yet, the name Castin still clings to the peninsula where she opened her heart to a young French nobleman, and the story of their union continues to kindle imaginations. It is said that she was buried upriver in the most familiar of places, the island of Panawahpskek. Surely the seeds she planted in her lifetime have survived the waning of many Moons of Ripening Berries. Somewhere she has descendants, and in their faces, traces of Molly Mathilde live on.

PORTAGE

In portaging from one river valley to another, Wabanakis had to carry their canoes and all other possessions. Everyone knew the value of traveling light and understood that it required leaving some things behind. Nothing encumbered movement more than fear, which was often the most difficult burden to surrender.

June 1938: The Penobscot Reservation on Indian Island, Old Town, Maine

Sitting in front of an open window in the kitchen, Molly Dellis Nelson stared blankly at the moon. Outside, crickets chanted, and wind rustled the leaves of the apple tree. Lost in thought, Molly heard nothing. On the broad pine table next to the window lay her manuscript about Molly Mathilde. She had finished the work shortly after midnight and had just spent a long hour going through its pages. To her surprise, the reading had left her wanting rather than fulfilled.

Molly Dellis pondered her mood. Ordinarily, nighttime was her time of peace – a neutral place between the two worlds that made up her life, an imagined space where she healed the breach between her modest life on the reservation and the lures of her cosmopolitan career. Within the unbounded realm of night's darkness she could gather up all that she loved from both worlds and rest in the fold. Or she could wish herself across the ocean to talk with Jean Archambaud, show him their daughter, and take solace in his assurance that they would all be together soon.

On this particular night, however, Molly Dellis felt no peace. She longed for Paris, but she knew that while living there she had pined for the reservation – for the security of seeing people who looked like her and for certain small pleasures such as hiking through the woods or hearing the steady beat of her father pounding trees into splints for her mother's baskets. She had come home to Indian Island expecting to fall into its familiar arms and find comfort for herself and her new child, only to discover that she had changed and no longer fit in those arms. Four years had passed since her homecoming. During that time she and Jean had written each other scores of letters about her impending return to France, but Molly had lost her bearings and could not bring herself to make the trip. Instead of crossing the ocean, she had gone back and forth between the reservation and New York City, leaving her baby in her mother's care while she searched for work – and serenity of spirit.

She had found little work and no inner peace. As a mother in her mid-thirties, she won fewer jobs in her usual roles as an Indian dancer, model, or actress. When she did find work as a dancer, she faced the same old battle between the American public's expectations of an "Indian Princess" and her own desire to perform authentic Native dances. The Depression only made things worse. It nibbled at wages until they became mere crumbs in the hand.

Most of all, Molly Dellis wrestled with indecision borne of fear and the belief that circumstances had robbed her of any real choices. Not a day passed that she didn't consider returning to France, but she was uneasy about taking her daughter there. Doing so would remove her from the place that harbored the last vestiges of traditional Penobscot life, and it would place her in a foreign land spinning out of control. Molly knew from the newspaper and from Jean's letters that Europe stood on the brink of disaster. In France, joblessness had soared and party politics had turned violent. Many believed that war was inevitable. Jean lived and breathed the tumult. Struggling to scrape together a living as a journalist, he tried to rouse public sanity through bold – sometimes dangerous – political writing.

In all of this Molly Dellis identified with Molly Mathilde – the two worlds that pulled on her, the conflicts that surrounded her, the circumstances that forced and foiled her decisions, and the gnawing fear for her husband and offspring. She had turned to this Wabanaki foremother for answers to these difficulties, and what had she found? An innocent, charming, and curious girl who had grown up to be a caring wife and mother, full of love and self-sacrifice. A woman willing to compromise in hope of gaining security for her family, her people, herself. A woman whose efforts ultimately had failed. Her husband had died an ocean away, and she lay alone in her grave in the old Indian Island cemetery. Molly Dellis could squeeze nothing more than this from the records. As she imagined her foremother lying in the earth, just a short walk from where she now sat at her own kitchen table, the sadness of Molly Mathilde's spirit overwhelmed her. Shuddering, she pushed the picture from her thought and reached for a half-finished glass of tea.

Taking a sip, Molly Dellis turned her gaze back to the moon and tried to collect her thoughts. What was happening? She had expected some sense of satisfaction and self-fulfillment from piecing together Molly Mathilde's story, but she had unearthed only enough to unsettle herself. The vagueness of Molly Mathilde's death, her apparent surrender to imposed changes, and the fact that she had never reunited with St. Castin all bothered Molly Dellis. They gave her the feeling that life, freedom, and love were arbitrary, that they survived – if they survived at all – by chance, not choice.

Molly Dellis winced at this thought. Suddenly she recognized something she had learned from Molly Mathilde's life: *she did not wish to be ruled by happenstance and uncertainty.* On the contrary, she yearned to take control of her life, letting go of nothing and reaching toward nothing without intention. She refused to believe one was helpless in the face of circumstances. She had finished Molly Mathilde's story – but not her own.

Molly Dellis realized now that she must return to France, despite the possibility of war. Moreover, she needed to find the continuation of Molly Mathilde's life experience in order to glean its full meaning. Already she had an idea of how she would do this. In her research she had come across a Wabanaki healer known as Molly Ockett. This Indian doctress had lived a century later than Molly Mathilde, and it appeared that she was more self-possessed and less yielding than the earlier Molly. She too had endured the wars and heartrending changes borne of colonialism but had guarded her independence and resisted every compromise. She had won a measure of respect and power among white settlers who relied on her for her knowledge of medicinal herbs. More than this, Molly Ockett was said to have had *m'teoulin* or "magic" – the ability to control unseen forces.

That night Molly Dellis dreamed that the Indian doctress sat at her bedside waiting for her to wake up. When she finally did awaken at 7A.M., she felt more hopeful than she had in years. After getting washed and dresssed herself, she tended to her daughter. Then she took the ferry from Indian Island to the mainland, where she booked their passage to France. The next day she crossed the river again and boarded a train for the short ride to Orono, home of the University of Maine. In the library there she began researching Molly Ockett's life. She devoted several weeks to the task. Then, in mid-July, she left for France.

Boarding the steamship that would carry her across the ocean, Molly Dellis held firmly to the hand of her daughter, who would soon meet her father for the first time. Glancing at the little girl, she prayed that the war expected in Europe would never come. A porter walked behind mother and child, shouldering the trunk that held Molly's belongings, including a folder of research notes about Molly Ockett.

CHAPTER TWO

Moon of Freezing Rivers

Molly Ockett (Marie Agathe), ca. 1740–1816

Late each autumn in Wabanaki Country, brown leaves
rattled in the wind while ice glazed the rivers and numbed life.
Beneath the freezing sheets, creatures languished: fish
hung in the water like driftwood, worms burrowed in the silt
among dragonfly larvae, and snakes coiled in the
banks for the long sleep. This was the Moon of Freezing
Rivers. It was like dancing with death while
holding on to the last breath.

IT WAS Molly Ockett's posture that caught one's eye. From the time she was young, she walked with her chin raised, as if challenging the sky. She had much to defy. Although her life began and ended in the age-old setting of a birch-bark wigwam, she saw startling changes in the world of the Wabanakis between her first and final breaths.

She saw her people leave their homeland one by one. Some were whisked away by diseases and wars brought by strangers from across the sea. Others tried to escape these disasters by fleeing to far-off places. But Molly Ockett refused to join that sorry procession. She clung so firmly to life in the ancestral domain that by the end of her days the white folks who had settled there called her the Last of the Pigwackets.

Pigwackets were named after their main village on the upper Saco River at the southern end of Wabanaki Country, which encompassed what are now northern New England and the Canadian Maritimes. The name Pigwacket means "the cleared place," and in this forest clearing alongside the river, generations of Molly's ancestors culti-vated corn and shared village life. Pigwacket was the center but not the boundary of their world. Each spring, after the Sowing Moon, most Pigwackets paddled and portaged their canoes sixty miles downriver to the Atlantic Coast. Setting up camp on a peninsula flanked by mudflats rich with the dank odors of shellfish and seaweed, they spent the summer months gathering clams and mussels, hunting seals, spearing fish, and collecting berries. In autumn they returned to Pigwacket for the corn harvest. After storing the crop in earth pits lined with bark, the tribe broke into small family groups that traveled to various hunting districts farther inland. There they remained until the Moon of Blinding Snow chased them back to their village.

Molly Ockett was born in 1740, during summer's season of plenty, when her parents were camped near the mouth of the Saco River. They gave her an Abenaki name, but it was soon replaced by her French baptismal name – Marie Agathe. On the tongues of her people the new name turned into Molly Ockett. The ritual of baptism had become quite common among the Pigwacket. Like most Wabanakis, they had a long relationship with "blackrobes" who had set up mission posts at sites along rivers in Wabanaki Country and in the St. Lawrence River valley in Canada. The missions offered refuge in times of warfare and often doubled as trading posts where Indians could get basic supplies, including muskets and ammunition for hunting.

At the mission villages Pigwackets met other Wabanakis with whom they had traded for generations – people from the Androscoggin, Kennebec, and Penobscot river valleys to their northeast, plus various tribes from the Connecticut River valley west of them and the Merrimac valley to the south. The fates of these groups were intertwined, for they all came from lands dangerously positioned on frontier territory claimed by both the French and the English.

Again and again, beginning a century before Molly Ockett's birth, the Pigwackets and their Native neighbors had been dragged into colonial conflicts. Most had sided with the French, whose small numbers and distant settlements posed less of a threat and with whom they shared a history of mutually helpful trade. They also shared the religious ties of Catholicism. These ties reached back to the seventeenth century, when so many Wabanakis died of European diseases that the survivors puzzled over the apparent failure of their own traditional beliefs long enough to consider the teachings of the French blackrobes. In contrast, Wabanaki relations with New Englanders had always been shaky. When it came to trade, the English were all business, violating Wabanaki custom, which called for gift giving and friendly interaction in all dealings. Also, these Englishmen were Protestants, and Molly's people spoke of them as "those who do not pray" because they did not wear crucifixes or recite the rosary – practices that blackrobes said were basic to Christian prayer. Worst of all, since the childhood days of Molly's great-grandmother, English settlers had been pushing aggressively into southern Wabanaki Country, including lands along the lower Saco River. They had felled trees, built sawmills, helped themselves to farmland, edged in on Native hunting and trapping territory, and set nets that kept fish from swimming upriver to Indian fishing stations. Year after year colonial inroads had increased until Molly Ockett's ancestors were being forced out altogether.

The Pigwackets refused to leave without a fight. With help from the French and other Wabanakis who lived nearby, warriors from the Saco River valley periodically raided English settlements beginning in the late 1600s. The counterattacks were devastating. Within a generation the adult male population among Pigwackets plummeted from one hundred to twenty-four. Time and again colonial clashes drove Molly's people and their Wabanaki neighbors from their traditional hearths to the distant refuge of French mission villages. For some, these religious centers became primary habitations where they lived between seasonal hunting or fishing sojourns. Others, including Molly Ockett's family, refused to abandon their land for long and repeatedly went back despite the growing number of settlers they found there.

That was how Molly Ockett came to be born in the ancient homeland of the Pigwackets. Her mother felt pulled to give birth there, even though the face of the place had changed and the air quivered with an uneasiness unknown in the Old Time. She knew the choice was risky. Like hauling a frayed net brimming with fish, things could fall apart in an instant.

Another colonial war erupted in 1744, when Molly Ockett was four years old. Pigwackets were deeply divided on what to do, with whom to side. They preferred neutrality, but they knew from experience that Englishmen did not tolerate such a position. Indeed, the English acted from the standpoint that "if you're not for us, you're against us." This time Molly Ockett's father and five other Pigwacket warriors decided to side with the New Englanders. Fearful of scalp hunters and struggling desperately for survival, they reasoned that a compact with the English might offer more security than their old alliance with the French. Accompanied by their wives and children, including little Molly Ockett, they paddled downstream to the English trading post. Presenting themselves to Captain Cutter, the agent in charge of the post, they announced their decision. Cutter escorted the group farther downriver to the English settlement at Saco Falls. There the Pigwackets listened to local white folks debate what should be done with them. Molly Ockett's father, who knew some English, tried to explain that his people wanted to stay on their own river and were willing to place themselves under English protection. The settlers would hear nothing of it. Having put their fate in the hands of these strangers, the Pigwackets had little choice but to accept a decision by English authorities that they all be moved to Massachusetts – all, that is, except the warriors who would be enlisted as scouts in the English army.

So it was that young Molly Ockett and her family went to live in the vicinity of English settlers in Plymouth County. They were placed at the coast on Assewomock Neck, near Rochester – a handful of Pigwackets in a colony inhabited by tens of thousands of English. Boston, New England's largest city, stood between them and their homeland, yet in some ways their days on the Massachusetts coast resembled life at home. They fished the sea and farmed small plots of land, and Molly's mother taught her how to gather shellfish, sew and embroider clothing, and fashion baskets. These bits of familiarity were small compensation for all that had been lost. The Pigwackets missed their freedom and the possibility of moving with the seasons. On such a small neck of land hunting was limited. They were dependent on white neighbors for various staples, which they obtained by making and bartering crafts. They were told that their way of praying, taught to them by the blackrobes, was wrong. The English called it "papist idolatry" and said the devil was in it, so the Pigwackets practiced their blend of Catholicism and traditional beliefs in secret. Most disconcerting of all, Molly and her folk were treated with suspicion, like trespassers. While they were relieved to have escaped almost certain death back home, they lamented the loss of so much that was familiar and dear to them. The adults, certain of nothing except their profound desire to go home, lived as though suspended in time and space. Unwilling to put down roots, they were in the place but not of it. Young Molly Ockett, however, was curious about her new surroundings and about the English people who lived nearby. She even picked up bits of their language, customs, and religious beliefs.

Meanwhile, war raged on in Wabanaki Country, with Molly Ockett's father and the other men from her village fighting alongside the English. They battled against their Wabanaki kinsmen and the French – former friends who had helped them and their forefathers in years past. As a result they carried a tremendous burden of guilt. They could not help holding back when clashes took place, for no honor could be won in those killing fields. When the four-year war ended in 1748, relief greeted the warriors like a spring day. Molly Ockett and the other children and women welcomed the men's safe return with gladness like none of them had felt since leaving Pigwacket. Now that the foreigners had made peace again, Molly's father told her that the family could go back home.

The return took longer than he expected. Finally, a year after the war's end, a delegation of Wabanaki Indians who had fought alongside the French traveled to Boston to meet with the governor of Massachusetts and request a peace conference. The governor agreed to an autumn meeting at Falmouth on Casco Bay, just north of the mouth of the Saco River. Before leaving, the Wabanaki spokesman asked if the Pigwacket Indians living in Massachusetts could now return to their own homes. The governor said he would not restrain them. So, when the time came for the conference several months later, the small group of Pigwackets sailed to Falmouth with the English representatives. After participating in the peace negotiations, Molly Ockett's family vanished into the vast woodlands and headed home.

Molly, however, was not allowed to return. She and two other girls were kept as hostages to provide some assurance that their people would not turn against the English. The girls were sent to live with English families. A Boston judge agreed to take Molly Ockett to live in his house as a servant girl. Beyond the political advantage of keeping her in official hands, he reasoned that this particular child, so full of curiosity about the English way of life, could be trained to be useful to his wife. The lady of the house, a stern, Puritanical woman, placed Molly under the wing of her hefty, middle-aged maid who did not appreciate having to share her tiny room with an Indian girl. Despondent over being separated from her mother, nine-year-old Molly quietly cried herself to sleep each night. Unsettled, she would awake in the wee dark hours, when all was still except for the low rumble of the maid's snore. Then she would slip out of her bed and curl up with her blanket on the floor; it felt more familiar than a mattress and sheets. But moping did not suit Molly Ockett for long. Within a week she fell asleep without tears and stayed in her bed till dawn. In time, her stout heart kindled kindness in the maid. Having no children of her own, she began to take an interest in Molly, correcting her English, telling her stories from the Bible, teaching her new ways of sewing, and showing her how to eat with a knife and fork. Neither the maid nor the girl could foresee how, years later, some of this knowledge would be central to Molly's survival.

While Molly Ockett learned the ways of the English, the Pigwackets pleaded for her return. One evening, eight months after Molly had been taken from her parents, the maid seemed strangely quiet as the two of them ate their dinner in the kitchen. Later that night, she sat beside the girl on her bed and gave her a bundle of soft fabric tied with a red ribbon. Pulling the bow and unfolding the cloth, Molly saw that it was a dress. "I made it for you," said the maid. "Notice the stitches – just like the ones I showed you how to do." Then she bent down and pressed her damp cheek against Molly's and whispered, "I hope you will wear it when you go home to your family tomorrow."

The next morning, Molly Ockett put on her new dress and said good-bye to the judge and his wife. Then the maid rode with her in the judge's carriage to the harbor and led her aboard an English sloop. To Molly's surprise and joy, the other two Pigwacket girls were also on board. The boat had nearly set sail before Molly realized the maid was not going with her. For just a moment the woman placed her hands on Molly's cheeks and looked into her eyes. Then, without a word, she left. The following evening at sunset the sloop docked at a trading post at Fort Richmond on the lower Kennebec River. There, the captain handed the three girls over to Wabanaki hunters who had agreed to take them to their families. Molly, suddenly as confused and frightened about being taken from the English as she had been about being taken from her parents, did not go willingly.

Molly Ockett's abrupt return to Wabanaki Country may have panicked her, but one look at her mother stilled her fear. Although she had spent more than half of her young life among the English, becoming nearly as familiar with their customs as with her own, she soon realized that she had come back to her true home. During the next half-decade, as she emerged into womanhood, she and her people enjoyed a welcome break from the perils of war. They spent much of each year inland along the Androscoggin River, a relatively safe distance from the pressures of English settlers pushing ever deeper into Wabanaki territory. This area, the first river valley immediately east of Saco, offered ample fish and game, and for a brief time the old ways flourished. Quickly, Molly Ockett learned the land, its wildlife, and its plants and their healing secrets. She also garnered age-old skills – snaring birds, hunting small game, tanning hides, and using roots, barks, and berries to make dyes to decorate clothing. She discovered the particular gifts of nature that came with each new moon. And she came to understand that the character of every season could be seen in the river: its summer dance with sunlight, its autumn face on fire with reflection, its frozen winter stillness, and its dramatic spring breakup when every crash of ice called forth a new bud that tempted one to laugh at death.

Following age-old tradition, Molly Ockett's family still passed the summer months at the coast. On one of many fingers of land jutting into the sea, they built their wigwams in open spaces between towering white pines. For Molly, these summers were bliss. Often, from a rock-strewn beach near the campsite she would ease a bark canoe into the water and paddle her way to an offshore island to gather bird eggs or comb the glistening mudflats for clams and clusters of bluish-black mussels. These jaunts always enlivened her, for she felt completely free as she stroked her way across the big water. Here, in contrast to inland life on the river, nature presented itself on a grand scale. While the river's densely forested flanks revealed only a ribbon of sky, the great bay shouldered a vast blueness. The river harbored muskrats and beavers, but here seals and porpoises outweighing humans swam the waters. Just beyond the bay, in the distance, she often spotted whales that looked to be the size of islands, blowing great puffs of water high into the air. Warmed by sunlight and cooled by moist wind scented with salt and seaweed, Molly Ockett dipped and pulled her paddle through the water. With the swish of each stroke and the slap of the canoe against the swells, she called up a rhythm that spoke of her grandmothers and all lost ancestors. Nearing an island cove, she glided over a kelp forest and maneuvered her boat alongside a tumble of granite boulders frosted with algae. Stepping gingerly onto the slick rocks, she pulled the canoe by its snout and guided it into a niche padded with rockweed. Here, with the tide ebbing, the boat would be secure while she searched the shore for eider eggs. She always stayed as long as possible – until her footprints, dark dents in the smooth, pale sand, began to fade with the returning tide.

As sure as the ebb and flow of the tide, yet another colonial war between the French and English shattered the Pigwackets' peaceful life along the Androscoggin River. It began in 1755, Molly Ockett's fifteenth year. Again her people tried to stay neutral. They wanted nothing to do with this war, but the English, unwilling to listen to Molly's father, who begged to be left in peace, launched a brutal campaign against all Wabanakis. They reissued bounties for scalps and prisoners and sent troops on seek-and-destroy expeditions to Indian camps. Soon, scalp prices soared to one hundred pounds apiece, nearly as high as a common soldier's annual pay. On top of this, a deadly smallpox epidemic spread through Wabanaki Country. Diminished by disease and terrified by the price on their heads, Molly Ockett's family had no choice but to retreat with other Wabanakis to Canada for refuge. Hastily, they left their homeland once again and headed north. After a long, rugged journey, they found shelter at Odanak, the St. Francis Mission near the St. Lawrence River, a four-day paddle west of Quebec.

Even in Canada, Molly Ockett felt uneasy. Warriors, returning from raiding parties, spoke of the ever-growing power of the English on the other side of the Green Mountains. They did not exaggerate. In 1759 France's defense of its colonial claims crumbled when the English attacked and conquered Quebec. They also raided and burned the Wabanaki mission village at Odanak. Molly, now nineteen, survived the raid only by crouching behind a bush. Secreted there, alone, she flinched at the sounds of bullets exploding from gun barrels and bayonets hitting their mark. She heard the screams of Wabanaki women and children and worried that her mother's voice was among them. She felt as if she had escaped to the edge of a coastal cliff, only to have it break off and plunge with her into the churning sea. Molly Ockett lost her parents, and the Pigwackets' French allies lost their power. Although the French would not officially surrender Canada to the British Crown for several years, the attacks on Quebec and Odanak crippled their political force in northeast North America, leaving little hope for France and her Wabanaki allies.

With nothing to be gained by remaining near the smoldering ruins of Odanak, Molly Ockett and several other surviving Pigwackets decided it was time to go home. They were small in number now, and, like other Wabanakis, they knew that without military support from the French they had no hope of stopping the stream of English settlers pouring into their lands. Still, memories of the old life pulled many Wabanakis back to their hunting grounds east of the mountain range. Resigned to English presence, yet striving to hold on to their own lifeways and independence, they once again took up hunting, fishing, and gathering in their old haunts. Ranging widely throughout the vast forests east of the St. Lawrence River valley and Lake Champlain, most Wabanakis camped seasonally for trade purposes near the English communities that were taking shape in their homelands. Molly Ockett, who already understood the language and manners of these newcomers was destined to fare better than most.

By 1762 land-hungry pioneers had moved up into the fertile grounds of Molly Ockett's old village at Pigwacket in the Saco River valley. Staking their claim, they renamed the place Fryeburg, but a name change did not stop Molly and a handful of other Pigwackets from returning to the place. Hauling their canoes onto a familiar slope of land alongside the river, they erected birch-bark wigwams within walking distance of the new settlers. Then they got to work preparing items for trade. In exchange for furs, tanned hides, and various crafts, they received ammunition, clothing, and staples such as flour, corn, peas, and pork, as well as tobacco, sugar, and rum.

Now in her early twenties, Molly Ockett had become a striking, large-framed woman. Her strong, angular features and royal bearing brought a certain drama to the array of native and imported clothing that she wore – her beaded moccasins, the loose cloth dress that hung just below her knees, the red woolen leggings embroidered with dyed porcupine quills, and her traditional peaked cap decorated with glass trade beads. Sometimes she crowned herself with a tall, black hat, imported from across the ocean, and this made her appear all the more grand. Silver earrings dangled to her jaw line, and bracelets jangled on her wrists.

Molly Ockett's personality matched her looks. She spoke with the bold confidence of those who have known and overcome hardships. She walked with the determination of a capable woman whose long, muscular legs had carried her great distances in all seasons. Her character and appearance caught the attention of many, including a Wabanaki hunter named Piel Susup (Peter Joseph), who married her soon after the English founded the town of Fryeburg.

By 1764 the St. Francis Mission at Odanak had been rebuilt, and Molly and Piel decided to visit the village. Like other Catholic Wabanakis, they were eager to see a blackrobe for confession, absolution, the consecration of their marriage, and for the baptism of their new daughter. They traveled the distance by canoe and mountain trails. Like all Wabanaki infants, Molly's daughter rode on her mother's back, safely bound in a cradleboard made by her father. Baptized Marie Marguerite Joseph, this little one became known as Molly Susup. She barely got to know her father, for soon after her baptism Piel died. Suddenly, at age twenty-four, Molly Ockett found herself on her own. Once again drawn to the familiar, she returned to Fryeburg and began to piece together a life for herself and her baby.

Gradually, Molly Ockett's self-assured and lively personality, along with practical skills and the cultural insights she had gained while exiled in Boston as a girl, won her a relatively secure place on the margins of the white community. Camping for months at a time near Fryeburg and other new towns in the region, she offered various services in exchange for food and assorted necessities. She fashioned the sturdy baskets and birch-bark containers that settlers needed for storage and harvest. She hunted ducks and from the pluckings made featherbeds. She gathered wild fruits and nuts for food. Most important of all, she collected medicinal plants for healing.

Unlike the pioneers who were new to the region, Molly Ockett knew the healing properties of roots, barks, berries, and herbs growing in Wabanaki Country. And she knew how to transform them into effective potions, salves, and poultices. When she heard that someone in the area was ill or had been wounded, she headed for the woods or marshes to harvest the raw materials needed for a remedy. She treated sprains with eel-skin wrappings, aches and pains with willow-bark tea, sore throats with tea made of goldenthread leaves and roots, poison ivy with a salve of crushed jewel weed or sweet fern, and infections with a poultice pressed from the root of Solomon's seal. For general well-being, she had her patients chew on flag root.

Although reluctant to entrust themselves to someone who was not only Indian but also Catholic, frontier folk often found that Molly Ockett was their only source of help. They may have missed the irony of this, but Molly did not: the individuals asking her to cure them were related to the very people who had earned bounties for killing and scalping her relatives and friends; the descendants of those who had brought epidemics to her people now asked her to heal them of diseases. How should she, who had lost so much, respond to a call for help from those who had done the taking? Focused on survival, Molly Ockett had little space for contemplating the dilemma of revenge versus forgiveness. She was a pragmatist and understood that doctoring provided a means of supporting herself and her daughter. Yet there were times when human suffering worked on her heart, and she could not help seeing her common humanity even with those who had attacked her people. Grace overcame her in these moments – as it did when she attended and cured the wife of John Evans, a former scalp hunter.

Molly Ockett's familiarity with nature's medicine chest gave her entry into the homes of settlers during their most vulnerable times of illness and despair. Sometimes, as she placed her hand on patients' brows to measure their fever, she tried to read their minds with her fingertips. She sensed their anxiety. As in her own community of survivors, the labor of every family member was vital in hardscrabble pioneer life. These whites were not a lazy lot, thought Molly, but they were amazingly self-centered. They pursued their own liberty while trampling her heritage and freedom, as well as that of every other Wabanaki. To weather their presence, Molly Ockett knew she had to be shrewd and self-assured. She held on tightly to these qualities, determined that she would not be a small bead on someone else's dress.

It boosted Molly Ockett's confidence to know that the people undermining her independence were actually dependent upon her for medicinal care. Doctoring won for her the tolerance of the settlers she tended and sometimes even respect and gratitude. She gave them some insight into healing resources secreted in the shadows of a wilderness still strange to them. More than this, her willingness to use her knowledge on their behalf tempered their nagging fears that Indians would attack and seek retribution for lost lands, lives, and freedom.

The fear of some settlers could not be stilled. They chased phantom threats of savages, assaulting Wabanaki families whenever they happened upon them in their forest camps. Wabanaki pleas to the governor of Massachusetts for protection brought no help, so Wabanakis lived in fear and suspense, aware that their lives could be snuffed out in an instant or broken apart stick by stick.

With each passing day Molly Ockett's people felt more eclipsed by the fast-growing white population. Most of Wabanaki Country now fell within what the English referred to as Province of Maine, which formed part of Massachusetts. By 1770 fewer than a thousand Wabanakis lived in Maine in the presence of twenty-four thousand European colonists. Whether they liked it or not, tribespeople had to befriend settlers to survive. Molly, always astute and realistic, reached out to many of them, in particular to the family of a Fryeburg settler named James Swan. In exchange for food, cloth, and other useful goods, she provided various services to the Swans and visited them so often that she became a kind of adjunct member of their household whenever she camped nearby.

For several years, Molly Ockett shared her lot in life with Sabattis, a fellow Pigwacket who also sometimes camped near Fryeburg and had ties with the Swans. Like other Wabanaki men of the day, Sabattis wore a mixed array of clothing: a European shirt and coat, red breechclout held up with a leather belt, scarlet leggings adorned with copper bugle beads and tied to his belt with thongs, and moose-skin moccasins embroidered with porcupine quills. He kept his thick, black hair short in front, long in back, and he hung silver earrings from large holes in his earlobes. During the several years he and Molly spent together, they had three children, but they never married. As baptized Catholics they could not wed each other, for Sabattis already had a wife, and the Church would not sanction a divorce. Even if it had been possible, Molly Ockett might still have avoided taking vows with a man who was just as proud, stubborn, and independent as she was. On top of that, she distrusted the fact that he drank dangerous quantities of rum – just as many Wabanaki men whose lives had been turned upside down by warfare and disease.

Whatever his faults, Sabattis was an expert hunter. Beyond feeding his own family, he supplied the Swans with meat and occasionally brought them delicacies such as the tail of a beaver or the lip of a moose. He had spirit and character that gave him special appeal and made him one of the best-known Indians in the region. Just about all the settlers knew him as the daring fellow who, early each spring, stripped down and plunged into the frigid river for a swim among the ice cakes.

Despite their camaraderie, Molly Ockett and Sabbatis had a stormy relationship. Puffed-up stories about their spats began to spread around the region. Settlers especially liked the tale of Molly's encounter with the wife of Sabattis. With great gusto they told how the woman came to town and demanded that Sabattis leave with her: instead of saying no or yes, Sabattis proposed that she and Molly fight it out. And fight they did – "like tigers" – while Sabattis sat on a woodpile, smoked his pipe, and watched. Some settlers said Molly Ockett won; others said she lost. Either way, she left Sabattis, weary and wary of his intemperate habits. Once again, she was on her own.

After several years in Fryeburg, the Swans moved thirty miles north and settled in Bethel, a new town located in the Androscoggin River valley. Molly Ockett knew that fertile stretch of river land well, for it was there that she and her family had spent several years following their exile in Massachusetts. After the Swans built their new log house there, Molly and her children camped seasonally nearby, usually on the north side of the river where other Wabanakis could be found. Often they set up their wigwam next to a Pigwacket chief named Swassin and his relatives. Unlike some Wabanakis who passed through Bethel just long enough to buy ammunition and have their guns and jewelry repaired, Molly and Swassin stayed for extended periods each year and came to know the settlers well. In fact, Molly Ockett's sojourns in Bethel were long enough for her oldest child, Molly Susup, to attend the local school for a time. Building friendly ties in the area, Molly Ockett did more than support her children; she maintained deep roots in her homeland. The newcomers could call themselves the town's original proprietors, but she never lost sight of the fact that Wabanakis were the true first landholders. She held fast to her right to be there.

Molly Ockett also held on to her right to come and go as she pleased. Sometimes her departures were purposeful – responding to a call for doctoring services or trekking off for seasonal hunting, fishing, and gathering opportunities. Just as often she left simply to get away from small-town boredom and the bothersome impositions of sedentary townsfolk – to reclaim her liberty, to find a remote place where she and her family could camp for a while beyond the shadows of immovable houses, the babble of English, and the grind and growl of sawmills. They traveled the familiar woodlands between settlements on foot and by canoe, usually ranging within an eighty-mile radius of Bethel. Sitting by a campfire in the depth of the forest, Molly could hear the voices of her foremothers in the wind. The dead whispered in her ears and watched through her eyes. Inhabiting her, they came alive – and so did she. In such moments, unspoken vows stirred within her: she would not be a ghost wandering in the land of the forgotten. She would claim her independence and live what appeared to be lost. Freedom belonged to her and she to it. She believed this as surely as she believed that she could reach out and touch the dark furrowed trunk of a hemlock tree.

At least once a year, Molly Ockett made the 160-mile journey from Bethel, north to the rebuilt blackrobe mission at Odanak for confession and holy sacraments. While there she usually sold furs acquired from her own hunting and from fellow Wabanakis who often paid for her doctoring services with pelts. One year, after earning forty shillings at the Odanak trading post, she went to the old priest to seek absolution of her sins and the release of her dead husband Piel from purgatory. When the priest told her that the fulfillment of her wishes would require every bit of her money, Molly reluctantly placed her forty shillings on the table. After the father absolved her sins and offered prayers for Piel, she asked the status of her husband's soul. The priest declared him safely delivered from the bonds of purgatory. Molly Ockett pressed the blackrobe, asking him if he was absolutely certain of this. He assured her that he was, whereupon she snatched her money off the table. With equal swiftness, the priest threatened to remand Piel's soul back to purgatory. Unfazed, Molly retorted, "My husband is too clever for that. When we used to cruise the woods, if he chanced to fall into a bad place, he always stuck up a stake that he might never be caught there any more." Convinced of her man's well-being, she went on her way with forty shillings in her fist and grinning to herself.

In the 1770s, when Molly Ockett was in her early thirties, a white man named Henry Tufts stumbled into her camp near Bethel seeking treatment for a serious knife wound. Seeing the gravity of his condition, Molly settled the young stranger on a bed of soft spruce boughs and bear skins in a birch-bark wigwam and took care of him. Years later he recalled his time with her and wrote a description of her treatment:

She was alert in her devoirs and supplied me for present consumption with a large variety of roots, herbs, barks, and other materials. I did not much like even the looks of them . . . ; however, I took the budget with particular directions for the use of each ingredient. My kind doctress visited me daily bringing new medicinal supplies . . . [and] I continued to swallow with becoming submission every potion she prescribed. Her means had a timely and beneficial effect since, from the use of them, I gathered strength so rapidly that in two months I could visit about with comfort.

This white man had done nothing in his life to warrant Molly Ockett's kindness. A true charlatan, Tufts boasted a checkered career as a thief, an unfruitful farmer, a deserting soldier, phony fortuneteller, quack itinerant preacher, and philandering husband. While under Molly's care, he saw that she made good money from her healing practice, and he determined to become her apprentice. For three years after his recovery, Molly Ockett allowed him to tag along when she went out to gather herbs or to visit the sick. Yet, despite a general willingness to share medicinal knowledge, she guarded zealously some aspects of her practice. After all, it was her last remaining possession and her primary livelihood. Also, like other Wabanaki doctors, she believed that if she disclosed her cures too freely, the herbs would lose their potency. Frustrated by this selective secrecy, Tufts tried to weaken Molly's resolve by giving her rum, but she still refused to reveal the names and virtues of many medicines.

Tufts was not the only person to make demands on Molly Ockett. On one occasion, a destitute settler from Fryeburg came to her Bethel camp to ask for a loan. After scolding him for trying to borrow from "a poor Indian despised by white people," she gave him eight pounds – a considerable sum in those days – and made him promise to return the next winter to hunt furs in order to repay her. This he did, in contrast to many less fair-minded folk. Time and again, Molly Ockett tried to call up the balance of give and take, but almost invariably settlers focused only on their own needs. They wanted her to see their plight and relieve their pain, yet they turned a blind eye to the fact that her way of life was unraveling right in front of them. As they saw it, it was her job to adjust to them and their habits. Remarkably, however much anger or frustration she felt toward colonists who pursued their own happiness at the expense of her people, she repeatedly acted on their behalf as a healer and even a peacemaker.

In 1775 the American Revolution erupted. It worried Molly Ockett that the English, after defeating their French enemies, could not hold peace, even among themselves. Wabanakis on the New England frontier were divided over this war. Some sided with the British Loyalists, others with the American rebels fighting for independence. Molly and some of her companions from the old village of Pigwacket chose the rebel side. In fact, three Pigwackets in her circle fought in the revolutionary army and received military titles. Several others, however, embittered by the impositions of settlers on their lives, supported the British. Among these was Chief Tomhegan, who hailed originally from the upper Saco River. In 1781 he and a small party of Wabanakis from Odanak, well-armed and smeared with red war paint, raided a string of small white towns on the upper Androscoggin River, including Bethel. They plundered several houses, killed and scalped three men, and took three captives. Then, before heading north to claim the bounty offered by the British for each American scalp or prisoner, they decided to get one more victim: Colonel Clark, a Bostonian who kept a hunting camp in the area and came there yearly to trade furs. When Molly Ockett learned of Clark's impending doom, she ran several miles through the woods to warn him. This was more than a goodwill gesture. She knew that if Clark were killed, she and other Wabanakis would eventually pay for Tomhegan's foolhardy raid. The colonel escaped just in time. Enormously grateful to Molly, he offered her a reward. She refused, certain that Clark's indebtedness was the best prize she could have.

After eight years of fighting, the American Revolution ended in 1783, and thousands of new homesteaders poured into Maine, especially into the fertile valleys of the Saco, Androscoggin, and Kennebec Rivers. The State of Massachusetts, which still included Maine, offered land to white settlers who had helped fight for independence. By 1785, when Molly Ockett turned forty-five years old, she could count for each year of her life a soldier who had received a land grant in Bethel. How, she wondered, did people give away something that did not belong to them?

The Massachusetts government also "rewarded" two of the Wabanaki tribes that had fought beside them in the war. In 1786 officials signed a treaty with the Penobscots in central Maine, promising the tribe modest annuities and marking off a portion of aboriginal land as a reservation. In 1794 Indians at Passamaquoddy Bay were given a similar arrangement, but the Pigwackets and other Wabanakis in western Maine were left empty-handed. The land that had always been theirs was considered too valuable to be left to Indian hunters; Americans hoped to capitalize on the agricultural potential of the fertile region themselves.

Although they held no official titles to land, Molly Ockett and some of her folk continued to steer their canoes along ancient waterways, winding through the forests they knew so well and stopping at regular campsites in the northern New England. Camping for weeks at a time near white communities, they still traded crafts or labor for food, tobacco, alcohol, and other goods. But all too often they were treated as if they were trespassers. In town they could feel suspicious eyes follow their every step. Molly continued to fare better than most Wabanakis. She had forged relationships with settlers to ensure the well-being of herself and her children. In Bethel, which remained her most frequent stopover, she befriended the Chapmans and the Bartletts, as well as the Swans; in Poland Spring, the Rickers; in Andover, the Merrills, whose baby she midwifed in 1790; and in Newry, Martha Russell Fifield, whom she had taught how to make traditional dyes, medicines, and root beer. By the late eighteenth century, most of these families had replaced their original log dwellings with large frame houses. Molly frequently took her meals in their kitchens, but she never stayed overnight. To sleep, one needs peace of mind, and that could be found only in her own camp.

The religious beliefs of the English had long fascinated Molly Ockett, and in Bethel she sometimes attended and spoke at Methodist church services led by the Reverend Eliphaz Chapman. She described Methodists as "drefful clever folks" but had little interest in patterning herself after them. Rather, she followed her own peculiar ilk, blending traditional beliefs with Catholic rituals such as confession, and occasionally adding a twist of Protestantism. Doggedly independent, she claimed personal veto power over the rules of all faiths. Settlers in Bethel often told a story that reveals Molly's maverick spirit and her own idea of what it meant to "keep the Sabbath holy." Just after daybreak one Monday morning, she brought a pail of blueberries to the Reverend Chapman's wife. Marveling at the freshness of the fruit, Mrs. Chapman guessed that Molly had gone picking on Sunday and chastised her for breaking the Sabbath. Insulted, and sick of instructions on "proper" living, Molly stomped out of the house. Several days later, she returned, not to apologize, but to reproach the reverend's wife. Her voice shook with defiance as she blurted out, "Choke me, but I was right in picking the blueberries on Sunday. It was so pleasant and I was so happy that the Great Spirit had provided them for me!"

Beyond defying the religious self-righteousness of settlers, Molly Ockett spurned their sedentary ways and disregarded their claims to her ancestral domains. She kept up her habit of shifting with the seasons – hunting and gathering, roaming the region at will, and camping wherever she felt like it. Precious movement! It gave her a feeling of unburdened freedom, plus a sense of oneness with treasured tradition. Like all creatures on the move, she could vanish as suddenly and unexpectedly as she had appeared. Signs of her fleeting presence – a wigwam, a basket, a story, a recovered patient – announced: This is where I've been and will return; these are the ancient trails and camping grounds of my people; this is our homeland, ours by birthright and by the Great Spirit's promise.

During her lifetime, Molly Ockett saw other Wabanakis give up hope of ever regaining their beautiful lands. They surrendered their vast hunting grounds in the face of pressure and frustration, or they sold them for a pittance for short-term survival. Surrounded by growing numbers of settlers, and having no nearby Wabanaki friends with whom to share their sorrows and joys, the few surviving Indian families gradually withdrew to the St. Francis Mission at Odanak or joined the Penobscots or Passamaquoddies at their reservation villages.

Molly Ockett refused to leave her homeland, and she held on to her practice, even after Bethel grew to eighty families and invited a white doctor to live in the community. It soon became clear that, given a choice, most folks preferred being tended by their own kind. Dr. Carter, traveling on horseback to treat patients as far as fifty miles from Bethel, cut into Molly's business. Although she covered a wider territory than Carter and continued her practice as best she could, it became increasingly tough to survive. In the winter of her sixtieth year, she came close to starvation while camping with other Indians on the Upper Missisquoi River in Troy, Vermont. To get by, they made and traded baskets and birch-bark cups and pails with several pioneer families who had moved there; but the settlers were also struggling, and the two groups weighed their difficulties against one another. When the white children came down with dysentery, Molly Ockett cured them but refused to reveal the secrets of her medicine. The following year, when her supplies reached an all-time low, one of Troy's settlers gave her a chunk of pork, and she expressed thanks by sharing her dysentery cure – a concentrated tea made with inner spruce bark.

In many ways it would have been easier for Molly Ockett to follow the footsteps of other exiled Wabanakis or surrender her heritage and adopt the ways of the white community. She toyed with this idea in her mid-sixties: after an especially trying winter, she accepted Colonel Clark's repeated offers to repay her for saving his life and agreed to stay with his family in Boston.

How the city had grown since she had lived there in the old judge's household more than a half-century earlier! Now, endless walls of townhouses lined a web of streets that seemed dangerously crowded with people, carts, horses, and carriages. This was an unsettling place, and the colonel's house gave no refuge. Its many rooms left Molly Ockett feeling empty, as if whole chambers of her soul were uninhabited. She missed the vast green forest lit with dappled sunlight and carpeted with sweet fern, jewel weed, and tiny star flowers; she craved the scents of pine, honeysuckle, and damp earth under fallen leaves; and she longed to hear whistling wind and birds frolicking in the trees. Clark's brick home suffocated her senses until she could bear it no longer and asked him to take her back to the Androscoggin River valley. Clark honored Molly's wish and had a riverside wigwam built for her in a small forest clearing by the falls at Rumford. Here, where mist rode the Androscoggin's broad green back, she could sit on one of nature's grand granite chairs, cushioned with moss, and watch the river tumble toward the wide embarace of mountains. She would never try urban life again.

Molly Ockett did not stay put in Rumford. She continued her wanderings – walking long distances in all kinds of weather, setting up camp in this place and that, offering her doctoring services in growing white communities that had less and less tolerance for wayfaring Indians. In the winter of 1810, when journeying south toward Paris, Maine, she ran into bad weather and sought shelter with several residents at Snow's Falls. One by one, they turned the seventy-year-old woman away. Exhausted and angry, she cursed them all and trudged on to Paris Hill. There, finally, the Hamlin family welcomed her into their spacious federal-style home. In turn, Molly healed their very sick infant, Hannibal, who would grow up to become Maine's governor and later vice president of the American republic.

Of the many stories passed around among the settlers about Molly Ockett, this one would prove to be especially enduring – in part because it touched on the early life of a famous man but also because it captured the ambivalent feelings most settlers had for Molly. In their eyes, there was something troubling about this Indian doctress who slipped back and forth between farmland clearings and dark forest wilderness with uncanny ease. Her devotion to Indian ways, coupled with her attachment to a Catholic mission in Canada, were hardly acceptable to most Protestants on the New England frontier. While needing her help, many felt uneasy about turning to a "savage" and "papist" for healing, and some saw it as a compromise with the devil. Molly Ockett stoked the notion that she possessed destructive magical powers once she discovered that she could gain an upper hand by playing into the fears and superstitions of settlers. She did this by punctuating her good works with occasional curses. Some of her curses spawned legends, handed down through generations in singing rhymes such as this:

> *Tis a curious legend.*
> *In my youth I heard it told*
> *How Moll Ocket cursed the white man*
> *When he stole the Indian's gold.*

In its entirety, this rhyme tells the tale of a settler who plied his canoe under a full moon toward a Wabanaki campsite on tiny Hemlock Island in the Androscoggin River, near one of Molly Ockett's regular stopovers in Newry, Maine. It was autumn, and the Indians were off hunting in the Umbagog Lake region. The settler pulled his boat ashore and stole through the shadows. When the Indians returned, they found that a cache of gold, along with other treasures they had buried beside an old hemlock tree, were gone. Some time later, Molly spied an ax from that cache in the settler's home. Retaliating, she raised her hands high and called down a ghastly spell on the thief, dooming him and all of his relatives. It is said that the curse devastated them: their homes were swept away by floods; the sap they used to make maple sugar turned sour in the boiling pans; women in the family died young; few children survived infancy, and those who did were mauled by wild animals or choked in their sleep from unknown diseases. Ultimately, the curse wiped the culprit's family from the face of the earth.

Although settlers passed down dozens of stories about Molly Ockett, almost nothing entered the record concerning her four children. One rare story that did survive shows that they, too, struggled with the newcomers. It is the story of her son, Susup (Joseph), who dared to fight back when insulted by a white resident in Carritunk, Maine. Susup's defiance brought him a swift and terrible reprisal from the settler, who beat him severely and then, shot him. No one expected him to live. Then his mother stepped in, once again as healer. The recovery that followed amazed everyone.

In the last years of Molly Ockett's life, Maine's population soared, approaching three hundred thousand. The relentless rise of newcomers, now outnumbering Indians three hundred to one, underscored a fact that she had understood since childhood: her well-being was tied inevitably and inextricably to that of the settlers. Yet she had always taken precaution not to become too dependent on them, instinctively sensing that doing so would turn the tie into a noose. So, even as an old woman she maintained her distance and freedom by holding to her migratory ways, still guarding some of her healing secrets, and occasionally calling down a curse on those who treated her unfairly.

In 1816, when she was nearly eighty, Molly Ockett fell ill while camping with Wabanaki chief Metallak and his small band at Beaver Brook, twenty miles north of Andover, Maine. Knowing that she had doctored and traded with folks in East Andover, Metallak brought her there, hoping that the people she had helped would now help her. The town contracted Captain Bragg to look after her for a fee. When Molly said she wished to meet death in a camp of sweet-smelling cedar, Bragg built a wigwam for her near his house and each day stopped by to check on her, give her a meal, and rekindle her fire. The time between his visits passed slowly. Living with loneliness day after day, she came to understand it and realized that it was the dark space between two worlds. It held the shadows of the familiar things that had been taken from her and the strange things that she had chosen to refuse.

This was not how it was meant to have been. In the past, one's relatives were not scattered. An old woman's children and grandchildren brought food and firewood to her wigwam, and she told them old stories at whatever pace she pleased. But now, after a few lonely months in a stranger's backyard, Molly Ockett died. Until the end she was self-sufficient; Bragg auctioned off her few remaining possessions and earned just enough to cover his caretaking costs.

It is a measure of Molly Ockett's reputation that many settlers attended her funeral. It may also be a measure of their guilt over the fact that their prosperity had come at the cost of her people. After a eulogy by Rev. John Strickland, gravediggers buried her in an unmarked plot in Andover's Woodlawn Cemetery.

In 1867, fifty-one years after Molly Ockett's death, the women of Andover Congregational Church raised money to mark her grave with a tombstone that identified her as the "Last of the Pigwackets." By this time, stories about her life and deeds had become legendary. Most told of a generous yet indomitable character noted for effective herbal doctoring, but some suggested that she was a witch with magic power to inflict harm on anyone who provoked her wrath. Over time, pleased with the local color Molly had provided and perhaps hoping to placate her spirit, the stealers of Wabanaki lands named some of the places where she had camped in her honor. Signposts popped up here and there across the region: Molly Ockett's Cave, Molly Ockett Mountain, Molley Ockett Trail, Moll's Rock, Mollywocket Brooke.

Molly Ockett's spirit will never be appeased by a tombstone or signposts, not, that is, unless the markers awaken some deep memory in future generations of Wabanakis. Surely, that was the hope of this woman who made a name for herself by holding on to her last breath while dancing with death during the Moon of Freezing Rivers.

PORTAGE

When making an unusually long and difficult portage, one shouldered the added burden of knowing that the return would be equally arduous.

June 1940: Royan, France

Molly Dellis finished writing Molly Ockett's story on the day the German army occupied Paris. Over the past two years she had pieced together the manuscript by fits and starts, hampered by the unsettled nature of her new life in France. During that time, the only sure thing had been her union with Jean – finally sealed in marriage – and their love for their daughter. Struggling through the Depression, the family had moved from one abode to another, always looking for cheaper rent. At first, they had lived in various Paris apartments, getting by on a handful of freelance writing assignments and Molly's occasional dance engagements. After the war broke out in 1939, they had moved to the coastal city of Royan, three hundred miles southwest of Paris, where they could share an apartment with Jean's parents. In time, Jean had found a job as Regional Boy Scout Master, which provided them a tiny, rent-free cottage. With the help of the older scouts, he managed the city's growing refugee center and assisted the local Red Cross. He and the boys provided aid for Jews and other refugees from Germany, Austria, Poland, and Czechoslovakia. As the battlefront advanced, they also cared for wounded soldiers.

Jean and Molly's days in Royan had become difficult. Jean's work earned nothing beyond room and board and left little time for the cares of family. Increasingly, it burdened him with stories of human suffering. Coming home late each night and crawling into bed with his wife and daughter, he whispered the day's woeful tales into Molly's ear until neither he nor she could bear another word. He tried coming to bed wordless, but the silence troubled them nearly as much as his hushed recounting. In a room haunted by the sorrows of so many people, neither Molly nor Jean could fall asleep without the warmth and touch of each other. At times they did not sleep at all, for some nights German war planes roared overhead and chased them and their little girl out of bed and into a shelter.

Hearing that the Germans had seized Paris, Molly Dellis felt all the more anxious, and the completion of Molly Ockett's story stoked her uneasiness. Each struggling refugee she saw reminded her of this foremother, as did every stalwart Red Cross nurse. But she had little time to contemplate the struggles and strengths she had found in Molly Ockett's life; German tanks were rolling toward Royan, and she and Jean needed to get safely out of town before enemy troops arrived. They had already applied for the documents necessary to relocate in America as a family, but the United States Consulate had refused to issue a visa for Jean. Now it dawned upon Molly Dellis that she and her daughter would have to find their own way to safety, without Jean. Their only recourse was to make their way to Portugal's coast where they could board the last U. S. government-sponsored steamship scheduled to take American citizens to the States. In hasty preparation, Molly Dellis packed her newly finished manuscript about the Indian doctress and shipped it home with her other belongings.

Given his reputation as a political writer, Jean Archambaud could not risk being in Royan when the Germans arrived. The night before the soldiers descended upon the old city, he said a heavy-hearted farewell to his wife and their six-year-old daughter. Then he and the Scouts boarded a small boat headed upriver for unoccupied France. Soon after, a friend drove Molly Dellis and her little girl to Bordeaux. From there, mother and child set out on foot to the Spanish border. En route they managed occasionally to hitch a ride – in a Red Cross truck, in a car with a war-time journalist – but mostly they hiked, hours on end, day upon day. At night Molly held her daughter in her arms alongside the road and sang her to sleep while German surveillance planes buzzed overhead. Within a week, they reached the southwest corner of France, passing within sixty miles of the site where the St. Castin family castle had stood. Molly Dellis slowed her step as she reflected upon what it would have meant to Molly Mathilde to stand so near her husband's homeland. Then she braced herself for the rigorous trek over the Pyrenees Mountains into Spain. As they crossed the border, she looked back a final time at her own husband's war-torn country, wondering if and when she would see him again. Then she took her child's hand, and they walked until they reached the city of Bilbao. There they caught a train to Portugal, reaching the port city of Lisbon in time to board the refugee steamer back to the United States. Standing on the rear deck as the ship turned out to the open sea, Molly Dellis stooped beside her daughter and wrapped her arms around the girl's shoulders. Fixing her eyes on the shore, she said a prayer for her husband, who, like her, was on the run.

Several weeks later Molly Dellis and her child made it home to Indian Island. Waiting for word from her husband, Molly stayed close to home. Each afternoon, all summer long, she walked to the post office, only to return home empty handed. Finally, just before the birch leaves turned from green to pale yellow, she received a letter from Jean. He had made it safely to a refugee center in southern France! Remarkably, he was writing from Pau, where St. Castin had spent his last years. From there, he and the Scouts moved fifty miles east to an army base and medical center near Toulouse. They settled in and began to provide care and entertainment for wounded soldiers and displaced civilians. Jean and Molly wrote to each other daily, as if an unbroken line of letters might span the Atlantic and provide them with a path to one another.

One day a letter addressed in an unfamiliar hand arrived from France. The penmanship made Molly Dellis pause. Opening the envelope, she pulled the pale blue letter from its mouth and slowly unfolded the page. The first line confirmed her greatest fear: "The present war caused many sorrowful losses." Jean, it said, had died of heart failure.

Numbness crawled up Molly's body, through her calves, her thighs, breasts, arms, neck, and finally her head, until she could barely move or breathe or think. Time passed. She had no idea how much, but all at once it was night, and she found herself in bed, fully clothed. She lay there on her back, motionless, eyes open but focused on nothing. Then, in the depth of darkness, grief rose like a wave, and she began to relive her memories of Jean. Now she could feel tears sliding over her temples and into her hair. Now she thought of their little girl who would never again hear her father read to her or be able to throw her arms around his neck. Now, exhausted, she fell into a fitful sleep and dreamed that her daughter tried to wake her with kisses.

For weeks, Molly Dellis walked about Indian Island in a fog. She barely looked at her child, who instinctively turned to her grand-mother for care and comfort. One day, ambling along the water's edge, Molly suddenly thought of Molly Mathilde, who long ago, perhaps on this very island, had also received a letter from France announcing the death of her husband. How could this be? How could her life be echoing Molly Mathilde's when she had determined to live like Molly Ockett by striving to take control of her circumstances? This thought sent her running to the house, up the stairs, and into her room where she reached for a folder she had left on the nightstand. She opened it and began reading through her manuscript about Molly Ockett. As she read, she realized that even though Molly Ockett had played the odds boldly, even though she had been doggedly independent and had compromised only when left with no other choice, she had failed to win the freedom and security that rightfully belonged to her and her people.

Coming to the end of the narrative, Molly Dellis concluded that it chronicled the birth of her people's bitterness. Certainly, the curses Molly Ockett hurled at settlers foreshadowed the resentment Molly Dellis felt now as she contemplated her foremother's doomed attempt to govern the course of her life. She felt sorrow give way to ire. Her darkening mood brought to mind a rancorous Penobscot woman named Molly Molasses who had died sometime in the late 1800s. Folks in the neighborhood still talked about "Old Moll," describing her as the bitterest tribal member of all time – and one of the strongest. As a child, Molly Dellis had seen a photograph of Moll's scowling face and fiery eyes, and it had frightened her. But at this moment the memory of that picture fostered a strangely comforting thought. Perhaps the fire of unleashed anger could burn the dross of all loss and reveal some hidden strength. With this in mind Molly Dellis determined to acquaint herself in depth with bitterness through the life of Molly Molasses.

CHAPTER THREE

Moon of Blinding Snow
Molly Molasses (Mary Pelagie), ca. 1775–1867

*Just to stay alive was an achievement during
winters in Wabanaki Country. Temperatures plunged far
below freezing and downpours of snow shrouded the
landscape and hampered mobility. Some creatures burrowed
in for the season. Others retreated to warmer climates.
Those who faced the weather head-on risked much. Often,
after the snow fell and settled, cold, wild wind
whipped it back into a blizzard. During the Moon
of Blinding Snow most storms had
more than one life.*

IN 1865 Molly Molasses was ninety years old and bitter to the bone. Most folks in Bangor stepped aside when she passed, looking down to avoid her hard gaze. Others, mesmerized by her keen dark eyes, paused long enough to drop a coin into her outstretched hand. Some gave because they pitied her, especially during Maine's merciless winters when she clutched a worn woolen blanket around the slope of her shoulders. Many gave out of fear, for they had heard that this old Penobscot Indian woman was a witch. Better keep her happy, they whispered to each other, or she'll use her magic against us. Molly Molasses fanned their anxiety with her volatile temper, convinced that their uneasiness propped up her pride and increased the success of her begging. To those who gave silver instead of copper, she offered a photograph of herself. She liked the picture of the stern proud woman wearing the traditional peaked headdress of her people. Along with the photo, she handed out a poem written for her by a local bard. The ode, "To Moll Molasses," ended with this stanza:

> *I write these rhymes, poor Moll, for you to sell –*
> *Go sell them quick to any saint or sinner –*
> *Not to save one soul from heaven or hell,*
> *But just to buy your weary form a dinner.*

Her life had not always been like this – just as Bangor had not always been the lumber capital of the world, cleared of trees and crowded with twenty thousand inhabitants from a foreign land. During her childhood, hefty white pines instead of brick buildings had linked earth to sky, and rather than the screaming of sawmills, the sounds of the Penobscot River had filled the air. Her family had camped often in glades all along the Penobscot between Bangor and the tribe's main village on Indian Island upstream. They had fished the river to its upper reaches and traveled its tributaries to fish and to hunt or trap beaver, marten, and other four-legged animals. She and her little sister had come to know the trails that snaked through the vast forests between these streams as well as they knew each other.

For a long time, when the French and English still warred over Indian country, this stretch of the Penobscot River valley had been a safe haven for Molly's people – a place where Wabanakis living along the Saco and Kennebec Rivers, as well as those on the lower Penobscot River, retreated when threatened by scalp bounty hunters. At the end of those horrible wars, scalping had stopped, but the King of England assumed ownership of all Wabanaki Country, and English colonists began pressing onto Penobscot land. The first homesteader came to Bangor in 1769, six years before Molly Molasses's birth. About the time she was born, two settlers built log cabins and a small sawmill at the falls just south of Indian Island. Others trickled in during the next two decades, but throughout Molly's girlhood there were more Indians than whites in the region. She grew up well versed in the old ways of her people.

While Penobscot boys gleaned the importance of hunting and warfare, Molly Molasses, like all Penobscot girls, came to appreciate the value of women's work. She learned how to raise corn and where to gather berries, lilyroots, fiddleheads, and waterfowl eggs. Her mother taught her how to scrape and soften animal hides and sew them into moccasins and clothing; how to fashion watertight bark containers and lash together a wigwam; and how to pluck a porcupine, flatten and dye its quills, and use them to embroider clothing and barkwork. Moreover, like every Penobscot child, male or female, Molly learned the benefits and hardships inherent in each season of the year and discovered the balance of firmness and flexibility needed to fit one's life to the variabilities of nature.

Perhaps most important, Molly learned about the Penobscot spirit world and *m'teoulin* (magic). As she listened to stories told by the elders and watched how her people lived, she came to understand that all life forms had a spirit force and that there was no line separating the natural from the supernatural. As for m'teoulin, it was a power given by the Great Spirit to a very few for the good of the whole.

Those who possessed it were able to contend with unseen forces. They could interpret dreams, drive off disease or death, predict where game could be found, and send a *bao-higan* (spirit helper) to inflict harm on enemies. For generations m'teoulin had run in Molly's family, so no one was surprised when it became evident that Molly had this gift. As the years went by, magic, more than the everyday skills of women, would help her survive.

At odds with such beliefs were Catholic priests determined to save Indian souls. Building on the traditions of French "blackrobes," Catholic priests from Canada visited Indian Island regularly during Molly's young years. In addition to giving religious instruction, hearing confessions, and performing marriage ceremonies, they baptized children and gave them Christian names. That is how she got her name: Mary Pelagie, which Wabanakis pronounced as Molly Balassee. Later in her life, white folks would make a word play on this and call her Molly Molasses.

During her childhood, Molly and her family centered their life on Indian Island, the tribe's ancient gathering place. This 315-acre hump of land sat in the Penobscot River, thirty-five miles from the coast, just above a waterfall at the head of the tidal river. Most Penobscots came to Indian Island each spring to plant corn and in the fall to harvest it. Many also spent the winter months here, but they left the place often, traveling by river to seasonal fishing and hunting grounds. In the spring, a good number of them portaged around the falls and paddled their canoes downstream to the ocean to hunt seals. They camped en route in riverine coves and sometimes stayed in one spot for a week or more to fish. Molly knew all the ancient names of their traditional stopovers. The names revealed what could be found in each place. Mar-tarmes-con-tus-sook (At the young shad catching) lay just above Stillwater Falls; just below the falls lay Mur-lur-mes-su-kur-gar-nuk (Alewife catching on the way). Asick (Clam-bed), near Stockton, was the first place they could find good clams on their downriver journey to the sea. The hilly place white people called Camden, Molly knew as Martar-kar-mi-co-suk (High land). Most years, when traveling back upriver at summer's end, her family camped for a time in meadows along the Kenduskeag (Eel River), just above its confluence with the Penobscot at Bangor. Beyond the good eel fishing promised by its name, this was a fine place to hunt moose in autumn and early winter. Continuing upriver, they usually stopped just before Old Town at Tar-la-lar-goo-des-suk (A place of painting), where Molly's mother and the other women painted themselves before entering the village.

When on the move, Molly's family lived in small, conical, birch-bark wigwams, which they could assemble quite quickly. When her father left their campsites to hunt, he slept on a bed of fir boughs in the open air, under a lean-to or a tipped-over canoe when it rained, wrapped in furs when it snowed. Back on Indian Island, they lived in a longhouse with members of their extended family. Several longhouses were arranged in rows. Men built the frames for these dwellings out of pine tree trunks fastened with spruce root, and women stitched together sheets of bark to make the roofs and walls. Inside they tucked bark containers here and there and hung woven bags from rafters and lodge poles to hold utensils, medicinal herbs, and other useful items. Like wigwams, longhouses had earthen floors, and they were furnished with animal hides to sit upon. In the winter, women covered the cold floors with thick carpets of fragrant hemlock boughs blanketed with bearskins. The boughs and skins, along with a crackling fire and a cluster of other bodies, kept everyone warm. Dogs, cherished hunting partners, huddled near the fire as members of the family.

Within most homes, an observant eye could see many signs that the community was not isolated. Iron pots simmered over the fire, muskets leaned against the wall, and canvas sacks of sugar slumped in a corner of the room. These items and many more came from trade with white folks. They had been available to Indians in the region for many generations in exchange for furs and, more recently, crafts. Fur trade was hardly the huge international enterprise it had been in previous times, for demand had decreased as had the population of fur-bearing animals. Nonetheless, Molly's father, along with other Wabanakis who had survived the colonial wars and the American Revolution, still depended on hunting and selling furs to eke out a living. Even the smallest white frontier town had at least one merchant who dealt primarily in furs, and there were always settlers who would purchase a skin or two now and then. Time and again, as far back as Molly could remember, she had watched her father go off with his gun, knife, and hunting dog in hope of bringing home meat to feed his family and animal hides to sell.

One of the best hunters in the Penobscot tribe was John Neptune, eight years Molly's senior. He was a member of the Eel Clan, which had a reputation for magic and for relying on eels as spirit helpers. His family, like Molly's, often hunted and fished along the Kenduskeag or Eel River. Lanky and agile as a teenager, Neptune grew into a tall, robust young man. His face was intriguing, for his features were at once fine and formidable: cheeks elegantly high but boldly broad; penetrating eyes gentled by sleepy lids; a firmly set, yet small and delicately shaped mouth; and a great beak of a nose that appeared almost petite head-on. In character Neptune was equally striking – a resolute fellow with a sharp intellect and dramatic oratory skills. Moreover, as everyone knew, he possessed m'teoulin. While this was quite common in his clan, Neptune's magic was uniquely powerful, so powerful that people said he could find green corn in winter and ice in the summer, and that he could make his voice heard a hundred miles away. From the time he was a young man, everyone realized that he would have a place of leadership within the tribe.

Neptune's commanding presence aroused the imagination of women. In the course of his long life, he would marry three, lay with many others, and father untold children. When Molly reached womanhood, her charms rivaled his, for she, too, was unusually handsome and astute. Her eyes, dark wet pebbles, shone with uncanny brightness in the smooth planes of her cheeks. Her generous mouth, set well below the flared nostrils of a small nose, turned up ever so slightly at the corners, giving her an expression both winsome and wily. Eventually, Molly became one of Neptune's consorts, and everyone knew that it was he who sired her small brood. They also knew that she was probably the only woman who could match wits with him, since she also had the gift of m'teoulin.

Of Molly's four children, only two survived beyond childhood: her son, Piel (Pierre) Molly, born about 1791, and her daughter, Sarah Polasses (Balassee/Pelagie), born several years later. Unlike their parents, Piel and Sarah saw white people often throughout their childhood.

Surveyors laid out the first plan of Bangor in 1784, and by the turn of the century three hundred settlers had moved within its bounds and a thousand more to its outskirts. Upstream, another two hundred newcomers settled even closer to Indian Island, building their homes in the newly established towns of Orono and Old Town. Most came because they sniffed the promise of prosperity in the vast forests of the region. For many, this promise came true.

Echoing earlier devastations of Wabanaki lands in the Saco, Androscoggin, and Kennebec River valleys to the south, settlers began felling Penobscot valley forests and milling the trees into boards and other wood products for export to faraway places. The Penobscot River itself held the key to their success: it offered a cheap means of moving logs; its tributaries served as arteries for carrying supplies northward into remote logging camps; and its magnificent falls provided sawmills with power to process the timber. Within a few decades, Bangor would become the center of Maine's booming timber industry. In turn, the landscape and the lives of Molly's people would be transformed more swiftly and thoroughly than anyone could have imagined.

Loss of land stood at the heart of this transformation. For years Penobscots had seen it coming and tried to stop it. In the summer of 1776 – one year into the American Revolution and Molly's life – Joseph Orono, the head chief of Penobscots at the time, had traveled to Boston to complain about settlers taking over Penobscot lands and cheating in trade. Addressing the Massachusetts Congress, he had offered to help American rebels in their war against England in exchange for fair dealing and a promise to stop the theft of Penobscot lands. In 1786, three years after the war ended, the new government of the State of Massachusetts reserved two hundred thousand acres of land for the tribe. Although it was just a fraction of his tribe's ancestral domain, Chief Orono accepted the deal because it seemed to offer security. He was wrong. Time and again, white loggers, hunters, and settlers trespassed on Indian lands, taking the trees, hunting the wildlife, and building dams and farmsteads. When Penobscots complained, the government in Boston proposed new treaties that called for giving up even more tribal territory in exchange for a yearly distribution of goods (such as pork, salt, rum, cloth, blankets, and ammunition) and a guarantee that the diminished Indian reservation would not be encroached upon. Repeatedly, hoping a new border would hold back the white tide, Penobscots accepted the compromise. In 1800, when Molly was twenty-five, Chief Orono died. It took six years for the tribe to agree upon a man to fill the traditional role of head chief. They finally chose Old Atteon Elmut, only to have him die in 1809. His replacement, Joe Lola, also died after serving just three years. At this point the tribe turned to Molly's old friend, John Neptune.

Now in his forties, Neptune was already an established leader with a far-reaching reputation as a dauntless orator and dramatic story-teller. Whether addressing a formal assembly of white officials or delegates from other tribes, or sitting under a tree spinning yarns about hunting, he knew how to enthrall an audience. His black eyes radiated intelligence and authority. Even in broken English he commanded attention and communicated vividly. He had represented the tribe in Boston and negotiated on behalf of his people in legal and political matters. On one occasion, he had even convinced a judge in Maine to turn around the death sentence of a fellow tribesman. Quoted in the local newspaper, his frequent public statements concerning the land rights of his people had found a bigger voice. Molly suspected that he used m'teoulin to balance the Penobscots' disadvantage. Certain that no one was more prepared than he to lead the tribe through difficult times, she tried to rally support for him among the women. Although they could not vote directly in the tribal council meeting, women liked to *boodawazin* (talk politics) as much as any man, and each had her own way of influencing the men in her home circle.

Some Penobscots, however, had doubts about Neptune's character. He was a self-willed man with an ego so large they feared it could work against the traditional role of a head chief as someone who was first among equals. With this in mind, they put him forward as second chief and chose the more gentle and kindhearted John Attean as head chief, giving him the official title of "governor." Attean lacked Neptune's shrewdness and charisma, but he was worthy of their trust.

Following Wabanaki tradition, delegates from allied tribes – Maliseets from the St. John River valley and Passamaquoddies from the eastern seacoast – attended the inauguration in autumn 1816. For this momentous ritual Attean and Neptune wore long coats of scarlet broadcloth, adorned with beaded collars and silver brooches and armbands. Visiting chiefs, also outfitted in ceremonial attire, offered speeches and belts of white and purple wampum beads. A white-robed priest read from the Scripture in Latin and led the congregation in singing the "Te Deum," an ancient hymn of praise to God. Toward the end of the splendid ceremony Molly and the other women joined the assembly and performed an honor dance, circling the ground in shuffle steps, accompanied by song. Although Neptune left the event wearing the mantle of second chief or lieutenant governor, he knew he wielded more influence than Attean. Molly and everyone else understood that, in effect, Neptune was the real leader. In fact, to Attean's chagrin, Penobscots and townsfolk alike soon began referring to his formidable companion as "the governor." It did not occur to anyone, least of all Molly, that the challenges ahead would be too daunting even for John Neptune.

By 1820, four years after Neptune's inauguration, Maine had grown to the point of splitting from Massachusetts. Gaining statehood, it assumed jurisdiction over the Indian reservations within its boundaries. Some three hundred thousand settlers now inhabited the state, and several thousand of them had planted themselves in the Bangor area. Penobscots, in stunning contrast, numbered fewer than four hundred, and most of them still moved about seasonally. Molly, now forty-five, often camped in the company of Neptune and his relatives, as well as with her own children or with her sister and her offspring. Her son Piel was nearly thirty now. A spirited and generally good-natured man, known for telling tall tales, he had an oddly fierce appearance owing to the fact that a man had bitten off a piece of his nose in a drunken brawl. Happily, his sister Sarah had reached her mid-twenties with all features intact. She had inherited the beauty of her mother's youth and all the finer aspects of her father's features with the exception of his mouth. Hers was full and sensual. Sarah dressed like most Penobscot women, but her comeliness brought a special flair to the usual scarlet leggings and beaded moccasins, the loose frock that she slipped on over ribboned petticoats, and the long strings of bright-colored glass beads that cascaded from her neck down her breasts. Typically, she wore an embroidered peaked cap made of red and blue broadcloth, but sometimes, like her mother, she laid aside this traditional headdress for a black top hat imported from Europe and adorned with a silver-plated band.

Moving about, Molly and her family usually avoided white folks in the same deft way they portaged around dangerous rapids and waterfalls; yet just as they paused at a falls during salmon fishing season, they camped near towns when they needed the goods newcomers offered. But town "fishing" could be tricky. On one occasion when Sarah ventured into Bangor to barter some ash-splint baskets for molasses and cloth, a prominent businessman demanded more than Indian wares from the young woman. When Molly heard that he had raped her daughter, her blood boiled. She hiked into town, marched up to the lecherous swine, and demanded restitution. He paid her off, but in Molly's eyes he had given no more than a down payment: for years to come, every time she encountered the man, she glared him down until he offered additional compensation.

Conflicts came in many forms but always pointed to the fact that Penobscots had less of things they once had in plenty, including freedom. Because many settlers hunted, at least "for the pot," if not for fur trade, the usual game available to the Penobscots diminished. Loggers took trees from land reserved for Penobscot use, yet settlers harassed Indians if they stepped onto a homestead to cut a few brown ash trees for basket wood. Most tribespeople had first-hand stories of being sold bad pork or wormy crackers from town shops, or being ousted from an age-old campsite, and many Penobscot men, flush from selling skins, ventured into taverns, downed some rum, and ran into trouble. Alcohol consumption among Indians and newcomers (especially lumberjacks, river drivers, and fishermen) had reached startling levels. Rum production within the state was 450 thousand gallons a year – nearly four gallons for every adult. Fueled by the liquor, even the smallest insult or dispute could ignite a fight, such as the brawl that had cost Molly's son part of his nose.

While Molly fended for herself and her children, Neptune tried to quench the fires of conflict for all Penobscots. He met with some success. When he traveled to Maine's state capital to meet with

Governor Rufus King and protest the destruction of Indian hunting and fishing privileges, he managed to secure some new rights, along with promises that old rights would be honored. He made public statements that at least raised the question of who was trespassing on whom. He lobbied successfully for a more sympathetic agent for the tribe, and he encouraged a charitable society in Bangor to improve the lot of Penobscots by establishing a special school for Indian children in Old Town. The school, like some of Neptune's other accomplishments, proved to be short-lived. It closed after one term, owing to a lack of funding.

Then, perhaps to boost his ego in the face of recurring setbacks, Neptune did something unthinkable. Ignoring all codes of honor, he seduced Chief Attean's wife, and she became pregnant. This breach of trust and the shaming of their head chief outraged many in the Penobscot community. Neptune had made countless protests against whites violating Indian rights, and now he himself had committed a serious trespass. Almost overnight he fell from grace in the eyes of many, and soon thereafter he began a self-imposed exile seventy miles away at Moxie Pond on the upper Kennebec River. Molly, no stranger to that region in her own travels, passed some time there with him, chastising and consoling her old companion.

While Neptune was gone, the Catholic mission built a church on Indian Island. To some Penobscots it seemed that the new bell tower and spire, pointing upward toward heaven, symbolized a rebuke to their fallen second chief. The same year the church went up, Chief Attean moved out of a communal longhouse into the first private wood-frame house on Indian Island. No one realized that his shift into a white man's dwelling foreshadowed a split in the tribe far greater than the break that led to John Neptune's exile.

The great breakdown in Penobscot unity began in 1830, at the start of a decade in which the tribe would face unimagined changes and pressures. By then Neptune had made peace with Attean and regained just enough goodwill to return to Indian Island. There was, however, nothing that he or any other Penobscot could do to alter what was about to happen to their homeland. During that decade the timber industry in the Penobscot valley out-produced all other areas in North America. Bangor, with a harbor broad and deep enough for one hundred full-rigged ships, became known as the "Lumber Capital of the World." Timber products milled upriver were rafted to Bangor or transported on the Old Town-Bangor railway, completed in 1836. From Bangor's expanding wharves, merchants shipped the goods to Boston, New York, and as far as the Caribbean and Europe. In turn, they imported commodities from around the world, especially molasses, sugar, and rum from Cuba, Jamaica, and other Caribbean islands.

One successful industry spawned another until textile mills, shoe factories, and brick factories cast long shadows over a river that was becoming heavy with sawdust and sewage. In Bangor, thriving businessmen built mansions and entire blocks of buildings – warehouses, shops, hotels, banks, and theaters. With improved transportation, people and goods moved easily and swiftly. Folks who had cash could travel by rail to Bangor, where they could board a stagecoach to Augusta and other inland towns or book passage on a steamship to Boston and beyond.

The flourishing timber industry also fueled land speculation during the 1830s, propelling Maine's population toward half a million and Bangor and Brewer's to ten thousand. The combined population of Orono and Old Town, next-door to Indian Island, jumped to six thousand. Every time Molly returned to the island, something of the familiar had either changed or vanished altogether. By the end of the decade, sixteen noisy sawmills disturbed the peace at the falls just below the island where Molly had watched Neptune and other men aim their spears at salmon with admirable precision. Lumberjacks destroyed hunting habitats, floating logs clogged major canoe routes and favorite landing sites, sawdust suffocated traditional fishing grounds, multistory buildings covered old campsites, and strangers – countless strangers – appeared at every turn. Molly feared the worst for her people.

With their traditional way of life so severely hindered, Penobscots found themselves cornered into yet another land surrender – their last. In 1833 they received fifty thousand dollars for one hundred thousand acres of land. The money went into a trust fund controlled by the State of Maine. In the years that followed, interest from the invested money went toward a school on the island, salary for a government-appointed Indian agent, and the annual purchase of goods that had been promised to Penobscots in earlier treaties. Penobscot territory, once several million acres, now totaled a mere five thousand: 140 small islands lying in the thirty-mile stretch of river from Old Town north to Mattawamkeag.

Molly could hardly comprehend, let alone keep track of, all the losses. It made no sense that vast stretches of forest were now off-limits. She was baffled when her son Piel told her that a settler had accused him of "poaching" and forced him to forfeit the large moose he had just stalked and shot. Confusion turned to anger when a farmer chased her and her daughter Sarah with a shotgun when they went on "his" land to cut some ash trees for basket making. When the Indian agent offered to supply Molly and other Penobscots with seeds and equipment for farming, Molly saw it as a ploy to get them to stay put on the island. She swore she would never give up her freedom, but a good many others accepted the agent's offer only to find out they could not survive on farming alone. In late autumn most Penobscot men retreated northward to Moosehead Lake and other wilderness areas to hunt, although even there the game had greatly diminished. Some women and children stayed on Indian Island, but others, like Molly, set up wigwams on the edge of one town or another and survived the cold months by hawking baskets and other crafts. When they had nothing to barter, they begged or bought on credit. Often, by the time the men returned from wintering over in the woods, the furs they had brought with them had already been sold by the women and the money spent. Those who had a good year were surrounded by others who had not and by the sense that their own turn at defeat lurked just around the river's bend. Gradually it dawned on Molly and every other Penobscot that they were being swallowed up by the dreams of strangers. For them the dreams had become nightmares, grim realizations that they were losing not only a way of life, but a sense of who they were.

In the face of mounting change and turmoil, Penobscot unity grew fragile. Molly could feel it and see it and hear it all around her. Many women, including herself, felt edgy, and their voices, once soft and lyrical, were often shrill. Men, too, were short-tempered – with their wives, their children, each other. Many lost confidence in themselves and in their leaders, and some began to question outright if Attean and Neptune were the right men to lead them through such difficult times. Attean seemed unsure, and Neptune, while as forceful as ever, had lost his moral authority. Attean may have put Neptune's affair with his wife behind them, but others proved to be less forgiving. Many felt that beyond insulting their chief, Neptune had become arbitrary, self-willed, and overly fond of rum; moreover, he had fathered numerous children with other men's wives, and he had abused the power of m'teoulin. A great schism formed between those who were fed up with Neptune and those, like Molly, who still felt a deep loyalty toward the aging chieftain. The conflict peaked in 1838 when Neptune's opponents called for a meeting to choose new leaders. Claiming that the time had come to end the tradition of chiefs serving until death, they intended to replace the custom with the white man's practice of holding regular elections.

They got their way. In the fall the Penobscots hosted a Wabanaki Confederacy meeting at Indian Island, inviting allied tribal chiefs and delegates from Passamaquoddy Bay and St. John River. At the gathering, two standards were raised: that of the "Old Party," headed by the well-seasoned elders Attean and Neptune, and a "New Party," led by Soccalexis and Orson, who were about half the age of the old chiefs. Neptune was first to rise and speak:

Brothers: we boldly come here; we face the storm; we fear not; for our hearts are firm as rocks that never move. Shall Neptune and his Indians give place to bold words? Shall he say, come, take his rights and power away? No, – never; for quite twenty-two years ago he and Attean were made governors for life; ay, for life.

Grasping for m'teoulin, the seventy-one-year-old leader found his power and wound his words around the audience. He could feel the crowd being squeezed into submission. Then he sat down and Soccalexis stood. Focusing his gaze on the visiting chiefs, the younger man responded with unexpected force. He went so far as to compare Neptune to a wolverine, the embodiment of ravenous evil doing. After much speech making, the votes were counted, and to Molly's surprise, Attean and Neptune lost by a considerable margin. But Neptune was not a man to accept defeat. Encouraged by their clans, he and Attean held tradition's ground and refused to step down. The old and new parties and their two sets of chiefs existed side by side, and so they continued for many years. Given the depth of conflict in the tribe, however, Neptune decided to leave the island again. Molly, along with some thirty other supporters, went with him. For several years they centered their lives in Brewer, across the river from Bangor.

The Brewer area was familiar to all Penobscots, especially to Molly, whose family had often camped by its spring when she was a child. Since then, hundreds of settlers had transformed the lush riverside into a new town, but Molly and other members of Neptune's small group set up camp on any unfenced site that provided firewood and water. Living in scattered wigwams on the town's outskirts, they made baskets, moose-hide moccasins, and other goods with which to barter. In fall and winter most men still moved upriver into the deep forest to hunt, hoping to return with a good supply of dried meat for their families, plus furs and moose hides for trade.

Whenever Molly had something to trade, she pulled her worn, peaked cap over her graying hair and followed a winding footpath through scrubby second-growth forest toward town. Most often she dealt with Jonathan Hardy, a white trader who had settled in Brewer during the early 1830s. Beyond his interest in buying furs, Hardy had an unusual curiosity about Penobscot traditions. On occasion, he even wandered out to the Indian camps to visit, but more often Indians came to him. When Molly or Neptune called at his home, he usually invited them in and offered them a chair next to the wood stove. After bargaining over this or that, the conversation would turn to nature, legends, or hunting stories. Some nights Hardy's wife, nestled in her bedroom, fell in and out of sleep listening to Molly and other Penobscots chatting with her husband until the fire burned low and the room turned cold.

Molly liked Hardy a bit and found this troubling, for despite his kindness, he was part of the reason she and her people were facing hard times. Sometimes, as she walked through the woods from her wigwam toward town, disturbing thoughts tumbled about in her head. What had become of her? Who was she? A sixty-three-year-old woman who seemed to have lost possession of her life. A woman with no husband. A mother who could not rely on her grown children to help her because they, too, were dazed by the changed circumstances that surrounded them. At times she felt as if her magic had been shattered – like sunlight that is cut to pieces by leaves and falls in fragments to the forest floor. She didn't dare ask her old friend Neptune if he had similar thoughts, but she had noticed that his spirit helpers were also failing. Perhaps they, too, were baffled by the way the enemy seemed to have two faces: one cold and selfish, the other rather kind and helpful, like Hardy.

Thinking about the future of her people, Molly came to feel that they had just two choices: give up freedom and become like the whites, or hold on to freedom and be looked down upon as poor drifters. She thought she had chosen the latter, yet even she had gone so far in fitting her life to the ways of the newcomers that she sometimes felt uprooted, lost in a place so familiar yet so strange. Unsettled by such thoughts, Molly turned her attention to the sights and sounds of the forest she knew so well: the colorful clusters of bunchberries and bluebead lilies, the songs of warblers and thrushes, the rustle of wind combing through the leaves and needles of trees, and the dull and determined thud of her own moccasins padding toward town. By the time she reached her destination, she felt surefooted enough to stand her ground, especially in the all-important matter of trade.

When it came to trade, Molly could match wits with anyone. If someone did not want to do business with her, she handed over a basket or some other item as if it were a gift. Sometimes years later, her keen memory enabled her to call for a balancing of accounts. "Now Hardy," she would say, "once we young we gib you berry nice knife; now we old you gib us fo'pence."

Sometimes Molly took her wares to the general store where it was harder to drive a good bargain but where the choice of products was irresistible. Heady scents of coffee, spices, and raisins permeated the room. Bottles of patent medicines, sacks of flour and sugar, and dry goods such as boots, clothing, and textiles, crowded floor-to-ceiling shelves. Glass cases filled with candy, tobacco, and other sundries tantalized the taste buds. Near the counter stood the potbellied stove and a great keg of molasses. This last item was savored by all as a sweetener for cooking and as the basic ingredient for rum, the favorite drink in the region. Like many settlers, Molly and other Penobscots sometimes made their own brew. Beyond distilling and drinking rum, people talked about the liquor a lot – its availability, its strength, its effect. One day someone, making a play on Molly's second name – Balassee – began calling her Molly Molasses, and the name stuck. In time, settlers claimed that she got the nickname not only because it rhymed with Balassee, but also because she used to knock on their doors and beg for the syrupy stuff. When anyone asked Molly the root of the name, she liked to smile slyly and say, "Cuz I sweet." Of course, if the name had anything to do with sweetness, it was only as sarcasm, for Molly was anything but sweet. Whatever sweetness she had as a child had turned bitter during a life of hardships.

One day, when surveying the goods in the general store, Molly picked up a mirror and looked at herself. The image startled her: an old woman whose deep wrinkles told only of sneers, frowns, and suspicion. Seeing that the corners of her mouth no longer turned up as they had in her youth, she placed her index finger at one end of her lip and lifted it, slowly. Then, inching closer to the mirror, she scrutinized her reflection, trying to see beneath a face twisted by disappointment and distrust to discover again the pretty girl who had known hope. Standing there, staring at herself and lost in thought, she did not hear the store manager approach. "Do you want to buy that looking glass?" the blue-eyed man asked curtly. Jolted from her reverie, Molly put the mirror down hastily, and the child whose face she had almost glimpsed vanished like a dream one fails to recount immediately upon waking.

By the mid-1800s, a fair number of Penobscots were farming small plots on upriver islands still in the tribe's possession. Most continued to feed their families, at least in part, by hunting and fishing, and they still sold furs, hides, and feathers to traders and shopkeepers. In addition, many made and traded baskets that farmers needed for harvesting and for household storage, but the profit from these enterprises was not enough to get by on. Of necessity they also began to turn to other means of making a living. Most avoided factory jobs where one worked fourteen-hour days for paltry wages. Some labored seasonally as loggers or river drivers. Men and women alike made and sold moose-hide moccasins used in logging camps.

Others took to the road and became entertainers in vaudeville and medicine shows. Molly marveled that white folks paid to see dressed-up Indians acting wild onstage. In everyday life, they mocked Penobscot customs as backward and snickered at the way she and other old Indians dressed; yet in front of a grand building in Bangor she saw posters of strange-looking Indians wearing a bunch of giant feathers on their heads and doing hunting or war dances. Right beside these pictures hung posters that showed white people sitting in chairs playing fiddles and other instruments, or play-acting in something folks called "theater." Molly, like most Wabanakis, recognized the financial opportunities of white fantasies about "injuns." Even Penobscot children had discovered that if they went to a pier, a park, or a train station and began dancing in costume or shooting at coins with a bow and arrow, passersby might give them a copper. Penobscot adults had found that showmanship helped sell crafts and medicines. Several of Neptune's children, grandchildren, and in-laws became traveling entertainers, making and selling crafts, and performing as medicine-show doctors. Molly's own son-in-law, Attean Lola, and her sister's son-in-law, Sabattis Mitchell, also billed themselves as Indian doctors. Traveling long distances by stage, train, and steamship, all of them set up canvas tents near wharves, train depots, and other New England crossroads. Some of the more successful Penobscot entertainers, such as Frank Loring, who was known as Big Thunder, rented halls seating several thousand and sold tickets for their performances.

The advantage of showmanship was that it paid fairly well and enabled Molly's people to move about rather than be confined to small tracts of reservation land. In a way, it echoed the seasonal migrations of their traditional life, except now they were hunting for audiences rather than for animals, and they had to make caricatures of themselves and their traditions to earn their living. This hardly matched the pleasure or honor of real hunting or of real rituals performed offstage for the well-being of the soul, but those who joined in thought it was better than wasting away or vanishing into mainstream society.

Molly herself would have none of it. Instead, she continued to rely on driving hard bargains for crafts and pressing for handouts. Her skills in these areas increased every year. When irritated by the way someone treated her, she arranged her face in a disfiguring frown, and using a voice that seemed to come from deep within her belly, she threatened to strike back. She did this so effectively that some of her own people even began to fear her. Aware that she had m'teoulin, they whispered among one another, "If she says you die, you die." Everyone knew better than to cross her.

Beyond intimidation, Molly Molasses sharply targeted her goodwill. Once she even told the white trader Jonathan Hardy that her son-in-law, Attean Lola, had stolen Hardy's moose hides. After giving the hides to Hardy as security for a loan, Lola had sneaked into the man's shed and snatched them back. Learning of this, Molly slipped over to Hardy's place, knocked on the door, stepped inside, and sat down by the fire. After a time she said, "You got dem four moose hide, Hardy?" He told her "yes." Several minutes later, she asked him again, and once more he said "yes." A bit more time passed, and she said, "You *sure* you got dem moose hide? Best you see." Hardy went out to his shed and found the hides missing. Figuring out what had happened, he walked a mile or so to Lola's camp and demanded the skins. After several denials, Lola gave them back. This satisfied Molly. After all, she had principles. Like other old Penobscots, she did not tolerate theft. Also, she knew there would be no mutual give and take if you did not hold up your end of a bargain. As she figured it, her meddling would help her the next time she needed a favor from Hardy, and it would surely win her some extra time in front of his warm hearth.

John Neptune, like Molly Molasses, continued to visit Hardy's place, even after he had moved back to Indian Island. Despite his scarred reputation, the old chief remained an impressive man, and many white folks and Penobscots continued to call him "the governor." A rousing speaker even in his seventies, he served several terms as tribal representative to the Maine State legislature in Augusta. When he was about eighty, a pair of local businessmen launched the first steamship made to ply the Penobscot River north of the Old Town falls and named it after him. Frequently, Penobscot youngsters scurried aboard and tried to claim free passage, pointing to Neptune's name on the boat and proclaiming, "He's our grandfather!" Given Neptune's notorious past, it was a just claim for many.

Prominent people knew "the governor," or knew of him, and sometimes came to his doorstep. Among them was the Massachusetts naturalist Henry David Thoreau, who visited him at his house on Indian Island in 1853. Now eighty-six, Neptune sat on the bed that filled half of his simple wooden home. He wore a black frock coat, frayed black pants, a red silk handkerchief about his neck, and a crumpled straw hat atop his head of long, still-dark hair. Although careworn and slightly intemperate, the old tribal leader could still charm a guest and spin a fascinating story. As he talked to Thoreau, several women gathered around the chief, including a third wife whom he had recently married. Neptune told Thoreau about his upcoming hunting trip and then regaled him with a tale about a time long ago when moose were much bigger, so much bigger that they were actually whales. It was a time when he, too, was bigger.

In the decade that followed, Neptune's mind and eyesight grew dim. One cold night in 1865 he dreamed that he was camping out and his fire had died down. Shivering and still asleep, he pulled his straw mattress from the bedstead and laid it next to the stove. Soon the bedding caught fire and smoke filled the cabin. Although Neptune survived that night, he died soon after of pneumonia. He was the last living Penobscot born before the first white settler built a home above the tidal falls on the river of his people. In nearly one hundred years of life, he had witnessed – and challenged – extraordinary changes.

No one understood this as well as Molly Molasses, whose entire life had been intertwined with Neptune's. In their camaraderie, each had built on the strength of the other, and in his death Molly could not help feeling weakened.

With Neptune gone, the blizzard of change sweeping through the Penobscot valley chilled Molly's bones. She wandered like an aimless ghost through a land she no longer recognized. *More white folks than trees*, she thought grimly. On a gray winter morning she walked to the water's edge and stood on the wharf watching the river leave itself. In the Moon of Blinding Snow, continents of clouds covered the sky, and the stream – on the verge of freezing – flowed dull and dark. Her eyes moved across the current to the far shore where crows hung in the naked branches of surviving trees. All at once they lifted themselves skyward, and as they disappeared into the storm Molly thought she heard someone whisper her name in the beating of wings. Snow fell heavily, and she felt its weight on her shoulders. The flakes that landed in the river melted and disappeared, and Molly wondered, *Of what can the heart be made that cannot be melted?*

She already knew the answer: bitterness, sarcasm, and detachment. In truth, these qualities were not the contents of her heart; they were shields she had set up to guard that heart. Now, in the Moon of Blinding Snow, she could see no other choice than to enlarge the measure of those shields and clasp them tightly to herself. With Neptune and all her other agemates dead, she embraced defiance as her sole companion. Hand in hand they walked the streets of Bangor, Brewer, and Old Town, shaking the self-serving assumptions of settlers that her people were about to become extinct. Wherever Molly went, she spoke her mind and acted as she felt. She collected gossip and threatened people with it. She demanded free passage on trains, stages, and steamships – and got it. And she drove ever-harder bargains when it came to trading. Molly Molasses became "the old woman people talked about." A shadow they feared. A dark wound exposed. At times she seemed frightfully rash, driven by raw feelings – or by spirits. Some thought she was mad, but what is madness but sensitivity of the soul at odds with cruel circumstance? Things were terribly off-kilter in this so-called New World, and in her last years Molly demanded the balance, telling people, "You owe me."

Ironically, she who had never wanted to market herself as an entertainer became something of a one-woman traveling show. An encounter with Molly Molasses was an event that bankers, lumbermen, and store clerks alike talked about around the dinner table with a sense of triumph, as if they had bumped into a ghost and survived. As if she were not human. This was the problem with the barrier Molly had built around her heart; it was also a wall that hid her soul. A wise woman knows this. Certainly a woman with m'teoulin.

Two years after Neptune's passing, Molly Molasses followed him.

PORTAGE

When spring followed a winter of unusually heavy snowfall, rivers flooded and shifted course, and calm stretches of water turned wild. Caught in unexpected rapids, voyagers struggled to steer their bark canoes clear of dangerous rocks. Surviving the tumult took skill and unflinching resolve.

7 June 1948: Bangor State Mental Hospital, Bangor, Maine

CASE NO.: 11,590
NAME: Molly [Dellis] Nelson Archambaud
DIAGNOSIS: Schizophrenia, Paranoid type, provisionally.
ETIOLOGY: Loss of husband in 1940; disappointing love affair; physical exhaustion; nearness of change of life; and unknown factors.
MAKEUP: Intellectually superior; temperamentally suspicious.
PROGNOSIS: May be favorable for recovery.
Dr. Hammond

The life story of Molly Molasses heightened the anger that Jean Archambaud's sudden death had awakened in Molly Dellis – the anger of being a casualty of someone else's aggression or greed. She had hoped to identify a secret and powerful strength in Old Moll's bitterness, but she had not. Instead, fury roiled inside her like a wild spring freshet spilling over the banks, drowning everything in its path. Bit by bit it swept the heart from her every endeavor, assuring defeat from the outset. She looked for dance work but ended up as a mail clerk. She wrote stories but never completed them for publication. She tried to love another man but met with betrayal. She sought serenity in her family's home on Indian Island but found that even there she could not sleep through the night.

Jarred from slumber by imagined noises and voices, Molly Dellis spent her nights pacing the house and mumbling to herself, or lying in bed staring into the darkness, anxiously waiting for dawn. Daytime was not much better. Her family noticed how she spent hours staring out of the window and how she often picked up a cup or a spoon and inspected it closely as if it were some rare artifact. They worried over her unkempt appearance. She seemed nervous, evasive, and distracted. Sometimes she cried for no apparent reason.

Late one night, her youngest sister, Eunice, awoke to find Molly sitting on the edge of her bed, holding a knife and trembling. Eunice asked what she was doing, and Molly answered that a voice had told her to kill Eunice. More heartsick than frightened, Eunice sought to comfort her sister, assuring her that no one would tell her to do such a thing. Molly quieted down and gave up the knife, and Eunice held her in her arms until daylight.

The entire family realized Molly needed more help than they could give her. She, too, recognized the depth of her need. Accompanied by her mother, a family friend, and the tribe's Supervisor of Health and Welfare, Molly Dellis walked to the ferry landing on Indian Island and boarded the small boat. The ferry master rowed them to Old Town on the mainland, and from there they traveled by car to the Bangor State Mental Institute. The pitiful task of committing Molly fell to her mother.

In the confines of the institute, days slowly turned into weeks, weeks into months. Molly passed much of the time writing. She made detailed notes about imagined conspiracies against her and composed long bitter letters that rarely made it to the mailbox. She also wrote in her diary, reflecting on her situation with an astuteness that would have surprised her doctor. She analyzed her physical and mental health, described other patients and various doctors and nurses, complained that she wasn't getting the attention she needed – and made careful and loving note of anyone who came to visit her.

For as long as Molly Dellis could remember she had kept diaries. In the past they had been her solace and her centering point, the place where she reaffirmed what was dear to her – family, nature, career, and the age-old traditions of her people. Through the years her diaries had kept her grounded in the face of a multitude of fears, from the fear of rejection and racial insults to that of personal failure and the loss of her culture. Molly sensed that whatever sanity she still had came from keeping her journal. So she turned to it daily, as if she could write her way to peace of mind.

In the safe, if pathetic, world of the mental institution, Molly Dellis chose to live privately with her thoughts and her writing, searching for her soul – sometimes frantically, sometimes with methodical coolness. She revealed little of herself to her doctor in their weekly sessions. She did not show him her diaries, nor did she tell him that she kept mental company with her three namesakes – Molly Mathilde, Molly Ockett, and Molly Molasses. She continued to contemplate the lives of these foremothers, lives that cried of personal loss and the withering of a people and their cherished way of life. Yet, for all their failings, each of these women had persevered in the face of overwhelming odds, and each had done everything she could think of to hold on to a vital core of herself and her culture. Perhaps more extraordinary than their personal losses was the fact that Wabanakis had actually survived as a people.

Molly Dellis recognized traces of herself in all three women. She saw herself in Molly Mathilde's selflessness and innocent surrender, Molly Ockett's clever use of defiance and compliance, and Old Molly Molasses's decline into bitterness. But she also glimpsed something that distinguished her from this threesome: from the time she was a young girl, she had reflected upon life in her diaries. As she considered this truth, it occurred to her that she would like to return home and read her earlier diaries, revisit her life, and see it in relation to the stories of her foremothers. She had sought the fullness of her own being in these women. But now she sensed that she was part of the measure of *their* wholeness, for at this moment it was she who faced the question they had faced: What of the past will be carried into the future?

It was time to go back to Indian Island and write the story of a fourth Molly, herself. She would do this not as an autobiography, but as she had done the others – as if it were someone else's life that had something to teach her about her own life. Tracing the history of her weary soul, she might stumble onto a hidden wellspring of healing, which, like the stream that fed the river that fed the sea, would replenish her desire to live and her ability to give.

7 August 1949

CASE NO.: 11,590

NAME: Molly [Dellis] Nelson Archambaud

This patient was paroled today, as improved, into the custody of her mother, Mrs. Philomene Nelson, Indian Island, Old Town, Maine.

Dr. Hammond

CHAPTER FOUR

Sowing Moon

Molly Dellis (Mary Alice Nelson Archambaud), 1903–1977

*With the coming of spring, the hard backs of Wabanaki
rivers cracked, and their crystal cries stirred a sleeping world.
The ice broke open and the streams flowed freely. Trees
grew hazy green halos. Birds winged back to sing their eternal
songs. And seeds, autumn's false corpses, prepared to
sprout anew and tell the story of life yet again.
This was the Sowing Moon.*

Molly Dellis cherished stories, especially Wabanaki legends about Gluskabe, the magic-making giant from the beginning of time. Stories carried the deeper meaning of life. They broke barriers of time and space, safeguarding insights and preserving questions until answers arrived. More than this, they offered relationships with people and creatures one had never met face to face. To hear and read stories fed Molly's soul. To pass them on to others – in dance, song, or word – gave meaning to her life. She had felt this way since childhood, when she used to knock on the doors of tribal elders and ask them if they would tell her a story in exchange for chores. When she was a girl, only a handful of people still knew the old Penobscot tales. Most often, she made her bargain with a wizened fellow who lived in an isolated corner of the reservation. She wrote about him in her diary:

My favorite storyteller is an old man, Hemlock Joe. He is a hopeless invalid and his greatest joys are woodcarving and storytelling. When he tells a story, he imitates the birds, animals, and legendary Indian characters. He puffs out his wrinkled bronzed cheeks and becomes Woch-ow-sen, the Wind-blower. He blows and whistles like the winds flying through the tall pines that protect his little one-room shack on the banks of the Penobscot.

One unseasonably warm Saturday afternoon late in the winter of 1916, twelve-year-old Molly Dellis ran through the woods down a narrow path toward the small clearing that was Joe's place. As she burst forth from the shadows of the evergreens, the smoke curling from Joe's chimney announced that he was home. Peeking through his front window, she saw him sitting beside the wood stove talking to a white man. By the way Joe was drawing lines and shapes in the air with his hands, Molly knew he was telling a story. She tapped on the glass, and with the flick of a hand he waved her in. Walking to the door, she kicked her feet against the house to remove snow from her rubber boots. Then she lifted the rusty latch and stepped inside. Joe, busy with his company, said nothing to her. Knowing it was rude to interrupt grownups, Molly took off her coat and began the usual household tasks, taking special care to be quiet.

While drawing up the bedcovers and sweeping the rough wooden floor, Molly Dellis eavesdropped on Joe's storytelling and stole several glances at his visitor. The stranger appeared to be writing down just about everything Joe said.

After finishing the floor, Molly pumped water into the bucket that served as Joe's sink and began washing the pot, plate, and the few cups that sat on the worn, wooden counter. Soon the dishes were done, but she did not want to leave. She scanned the room and noticed Joe's jacket on the stool near his chair. Tiptoeing across the floor, she picked up the rumpled coat, held it in the air by the collar, and smoothed it with her hand. Then she hung it on a crooked nail by the door and turned toward Joe, hoping he would see that she had finished and invite her to stay for another story. She waited quietly, and soon, with a subtle nod of the head, he gestured for her to come and sit next to him.

"This man's what they call a professor," said Joe, introducing Molly Dellis to his guest. "He's done a lot of reading, and he likes my stories as much as you do."

Then, to Molly's surprise, the professor greeted her in Penobscot. Never before had she heard a white person speak her language. Seeing her startled expression, Joe burst out laughing, but the professor gave her a friendly wink and said a few more words. Immediately, she decided she would like to know him for a long time. His name was Dr. Frank Speck.

"I'll tell one more story," said Joe, "the tale of Gluskabe and the great bullfrog who drank the river dry." This was one of Molly's favorites. She sat down on the old wooden footstool beside Joe, placed her elbows on her knees, and propped up her chin with the palms of her hands. Joe began: "Long ago, in an Indian village that stood beside a great river, lived a people who loved good water." As he continued,

Molly turned her eyes to the window. She could just see a small stretch of the river that wrapped around Indian Island. Struck by an early thaw, the ice had already cracked open, revealing a sweep of glistening water. As Molly watched and listened, Joe's words danced with arrows of sunlight on the water.

Her life began in a small wooden house next to the ferry landing on Indian Island, a 315-acre piece of reservation land shaped like an arrowhead. The house sat so close to the water that during spring floods the river sometimes flowed right through it. The oldest of eight children, she had arrived in November 1903 – in the middle of what old Penobscots called Winter Fish Moon. Soon after her maternal grandmother had pulled her from the womb, her parents had her baptized by the reservation's priest and gave her a Christian name, Mary Alice. But they and everyone else on the island pronounced it in the Indian way – Molly Dellis. For short, they called her Molly. From the beginning people spoke of her beauty – the graceful angles of her face, her delicate nose, rosebud mouth, and blackberry eyes.

Both of Molly's parents were Wabanakis. Her mother, Philomene Saulis Nelson, came from the St. John River valley. She was a Maliseet, with some Penobscot and French ancestry as well. As the seventh daughter of a seventh daughter, Philomene had a birthright that Wabanakis believed gave her special power as a traditional healer. Like most Wabanaki women of her time, however, her major work was basketry. Baskets were now vital to the livelihood of Wabanakis, and basketmaking was one of the few ways to earn cash without surrendering traditional life. Besides providing income, baskets were becoming a symbol of Wabanaki culture. As they gained prominence, so did the women who made them. Beyond her reputation as one of the finest basket weavers on Indian Island, Philomene was known for her beauty – a woman whose high cheeks never lost their blush.

Molly's father, Horace Nelson, was a Penobscot with some Passamaquoddy ancestry. Overall, his looks were fairly average, but his dark, penetrating eyes captivated those he gazed upon – women in particular. His keen intellect and passion for reading helped him become one of the first people from Indian Island to earn a high school diploma. He even ventured off to Dartmouth College in New Hampshire, but after one year, missing all that was familiar to him, he returned home. Back on the Penobscot Reservation, Horace married Philomene and pursued work that responded to the seasons – hunting, fishing, gardening, canoe-building, gathering sweetgrass and preparing ashwood strips for Philomene's baskets, selling crafts to summer tourists, and rowing the ferry back and forth between Indian Island and Old Town. He also played the French horn in the Penobscot Band for many years and served one term as tribal chief, another as the Penobscot representative to the Maine state legislature. His work habits were irregular, however, and his jobs rarely paid well. This made many hardships for his family.

By the time Molly Dellis was born, Europeans had worn down her people and their way of life through three centuries of impositions. Barely four hundred souls lived on Indian Island in 1903, and it seemed impossible that this small tribal community could survive much longer. Yet, remarkably, some Penobscot traditions remained, kept alive by habit and determination. Their presence hinted at a past whose spirit lingered in the air like the scent of pine. Molly Dellis breathed in deeply. She sought out the old stories and joined in ancient dances at tribal gatherings. She learned how to gather sweetgrass and weave baskets, and she discovered the rhythms and solace of nature still harbored in the island's streams and woods. By age ten she could address the stars by name and catch a fish by hand.

Although Molly loved Indian Island and its traditions, her intense curiosity drew her to the world beyond. She treasured her few books and longed to be a serious writer – a "delineator of life," as she told her diary when she was a teenager. To do this she would have to gather up experiences. So, after reaching the limits of the Catholic mission school on the reservation, she went to high school on the mainland, traveling there by canoe or on foot over the ice, depending on the season. Like her father – but unlike so many other Indian children of her generation – Molly vowed not to let the jeers and gibes of white classmates keep her from getting a formal education. Many times she felt tempted to break that vow. In grade eleven she wrote this in her diary:

The white boys of Old Town shun the Indian girl like poison, each afraid to be seen even saying "how do you do?" or tipping their hat. All thoughts of good are thrust into the background and thoughts of inferiority and evil tendencies are directed toward the Indian with little sympathy or understanding. That is why we admire and welcome as a friend the one who is not ashamed to be seen with us.

It was always like that when her people ventured off the reservation – here and there an island of kindness in seas of white disdain. Although Molly cherished the kindness, it always stood in the shadow of scorn, and this made her wary.

At a very early age Molly Dellis learned the virtues of hard work and selflessness. As the oldest child in the family, she was expected to bear some of the burden of Philomene's motherly duties. Beyond numerous household chores and endless babysitting, this meant helping her mother make baskets and participating in the women's sweetgrass-braiding parties until her hands were red and swollen. How often Molly told her diary, "Braided one hundred yards of sweetgrass today!" Helping to support the family also meant peddling Philomene's handiwork and baked goods door to door. When Molly left the house with a basketful of her mother's plump donuts, she sometimes spied tourists arriving at the ferry landing. Recognizing a sales opportunity, she scurried down to meet them. Occasionally, someone would buy all the donuts plus the basket, and quite often visitors smiled benignly and asked Molly and any other children nearby, "Can you dance for us?" The youngsters always complied immediately – whooping, waving their arms, and pawing the ground with the sort of exaggerated movements they had learned would win them a nickel.

Of course they knew the real dances, for everyone on the reservation still danced them on special occasions. They always danced at the chief's inauguration. What an event that was! Besides Penobscots young and old, Wabanaki leaders from other tribes attended the celebration in the tribal council house, along with white public officials who had been invited from Old Town and the state capital in Augusta. The chief and most of the older Indian people dressed in traditional clothing. After the ceremony and the chief's long speech, the dancing began in tempo with chants and the shake of a rattle. Young Molly Dellis did the welcome dance with everyone and the shuffle dance with the women, but the snake dance was her favorite because it had a wildness to it. Standing in a line, hands clasping the wrists of those on either side, they all followed the head dancer who led them round and round like a slithering snake. He moved faster and faster until the human reptile began to swing like the lash of a whip. Everyone kept pace and held on ever tighter, determined not to break the snake. Women and children, who always danced at the tail's riotous end, were usually the first to come unclasped. Then they would stand aside, catching their breath and watching the dance grow so intense that the serpent snapped again and again. Then, with much laughter, all made fun of the men who lost their grip.

After traditional dancing, the Penobscot Indian Band, which included a pianist, violinist, cornet player, and Molly's father on the French horn, stepped on stage and played several waltzes. The crowd responded, splitting into couples who glided sure-footedly across the floor.

From the time Molly Dellis was little she knew the dances of two worlds. She loved them both more than most people in either world did. For several years she even studied ballet at Miss Odiorne's dance studio in Bangor. She scrubbed floors in exchange for lessons, quite willing to go on her knees for an opportunity to dance on her toes. From the nuns at the island's Catholic school she learned to play the piano and sing. Hard work, talent, and grace led to solos at tribal events and in school. As a young teenager she won a talent contest in Bangor.

Molly Dellis's father always encouraged his daughter's artistic endeavors, just as he encouraged her love of books. Her mother was the practical one. In the summer of 1918, when Molly was nearly fifteen, Philomene thought it was time for her oldest daughter to use her talent to earn some money for the family. It was not difficult to find a job, for opportunities to perform were abundant in those days. Vaudeville was so popular at the time that the average American went to a show twice a week – more often than they bathed. Molly danced and sang with several Indian vaudeville troupes that traveled throughout New England. Originally, Philomene intended for her daughter to work only in the summer, but soon Molly was missing entire school terms. By 1923, when she was twenty, she had not yet finished high school. This bothered her greatly, for she had an intellectual hunger and cherished her education.

On the road Molly Dellis met many other Indian performers. Working in vaudeville, circuses, and medicine- and wild-west shows had become something of a new tradition among Native Americans. It had started in the previous century, in part as a way to market Indian baskets and other novelties. By the time Molly's grandparents were born in the mid-1800s, quite a few Wabanakis traveled around New England by stagecoach, steamship, and railway, to sell their crafts and medicinal herbs. Setting up shop at railway stations, piers, resorts, and city parks such as the Boston Commons, some Indians attracted customers by dressing in costume, setting up a wigwam, and weaving baskets. Others drew a crowd by tossing coins into the air and hitting them with a well-aimed arrow.

Best known among early Penobscot performers was a fellow called Big Thunder. Although Molly Dellis was not yet three years old when this showman died at the age of eighty-three, she knew about his adventurous life because folks talked about it long after he was gone. His real name was Frank Loring. In 1833, when he was just a boy, Frank's mother died, and he and his older sisters went on the road to make a living for themselves. They roamed New England selling baskets, and they spent eight months on display in P. T. Barnum's American Museum in New York City. In time, Frank grew to be a six-foot-four-inch showman worthy of the name Big Thunder. He directed and performed in Indian traveling shows for several decades. He became known especially for his production of the popular play *Pocahontas,* in which he played a fierce Indian chief as well as a convincing Capt. John Smith. By the time of his death, many Indians all across America had turned to performing and crafts for survival. Like Frank Loring, they were politically and economically tied to reservations, but a lack of work opportunities there had left them poor, aimless, and bored. The entertainment circuit offered not only a livelihood, but also a diversion from their plight. However, Indians who packaged their traditions for the stage or marketplace faced a problem. On one hand, their work affirmed the cultural distinctiveness of Indian peoples; on the other, the very act of removing tribal dances and ceremonies from their traditional settings and altering them to suit popular taste robbed them of their cultural meaning.

When Molly Dellis first began performing, she did not yet understand this contradiction, but nonetheless, she had mixed feelings about being on the road. Her managers were often abusive. One of them regularly placed her in a showcase for hours on end as a living display to promote his programs. Besides paying low wages, he required all of his performers to buy or make their own costumes, and more than once he failed to reimburse them for room and board. Such practices were not unusual. On top of these difficulties, as Molly jaunted from city to city, she missed the rural nature of life at home, and she felt lonesome for her family. Often she wrote entries such as this in her diary: "How I long to be home for even a few days to see the dear faces of my loved ones."

In spite of the challenges of road-show life, Molly Dellis loved dancing, and she took it upon herself to become very good at it. Even as a teenager she critically reviewed her work in her diaries. Although quite hard on herself – using such words as "stinking" and "poor" – she also made a note of it when a crowd gave a "wonderful applause" or "demanded an encore." Most of the audiences were white, and Molly felt baffled by the way they responded with both jeers and cheers, as if they could not decide if Indians were backward savages or noble icons of nature. Either view was hard to bear. After one show Molly confided to her diary: "Cried after performance. Why? Heard a cutting remark." Sometimes she fought back, as revealed in this journal entry: "A front row couple made fun of us. I flirted with the fellow and the girl became silent." In another instance, she challenged a crowd's insults publicly by writing a short article titled "A Criticism on Racial Feeling" and sending it to the *Boston Telegram*.

Molly Dellis usually overcame or put aside whatever hardships she faced. Sometimes she used them as material for poetry and stories she wrote in spare moments. Spurred by her passion for dancing and by the knowledge that her family depended upon her, she continued to perform and to send most of her modest earnings home. "Giving my heart and soul to my dancing and my career to help my family is my task," she told her diary. Most of all she wanted to make life easier for Philomene. "If I become famous," she wrote, "Mama won't have to make any more Indian baskets."

In the winter of 1924, after attending school the fall term, Molly Dellis set out on a tour of eastern colleges and universities with a company of Indian dancers. At the University of Pennsylvania she looked up Dr. Frank Speck, the anthropology professor she had met back home at Hemlock Joe's place eight years earlier. She had seen him on Indian Island several times since that first meeting. This time, he invited her to his home to have dinner with him and his family. Before the meal was over Molly realized that Dr. Speck spoke her language in more ways than one. He understood her passion for the old stories of her people, her love of writing, her frustrations with the way white audiences responded to Indian performers, and her desire to deepen her own insights into the meaning behind the dances she performed. Inspired by him to pursue her aspirations, she decided to study journalism and anthropology at the University of Pennsylvania. Since she had not finished her last year of high school, Speck arranged for her to attend Swarthmore Preparatory School for several months. Then, in September 1924, he helped her enroll in the university.

For a full year Molly Dellis took courses and worked for Speck as an office assistant. During this time she had several poems published, and she reached beyond vaudeville with her dancing. She researched the origins of tribal dances (such as the deer, clown, and snake dances) and gave several recitals in which she not only danced and sang, but also lectured for schools and social organizations in the area. This felt very much like a road to fulfillment.

Financial pressures, however, sent Molly Dellis back to the stage full time. When the Miller Brothers' 101 Ranch Wild West show from Oklahoma came through Philadelphia at the end of spring term in 1925, she signed on as a performer – prodded by her younger sister Apid, who had joined the company the previous year. Unlike Apid, Molly was offered a featured role that would earn her the fairly decent salary of thirty-five dollars a month, plus room and board. Seeing this as a chance to build up her "college fund" and still send a bit of money home, Molly said good-bye to Dr. Speck and stepped into the world of wild west shows as Princess Neeburban, the Penobscot name for Northern Lights. By this time some Indian leaders had come forward to criticize such shows as demoralizing showcases that degraded tribal customs. Molly quickly discovered why. Within half a year she quit, sick of a circus atmosphere that mocked traditions and starved her artistic soul.

After a respite of several months at home, Molly Dellis ventured to New York City in the winter of 1926, hoping to find more satisfying work. Now twenty-three, she had become a remarkably lovely woman, a lithe, dark-eyed beauty who wound her long black hair into two sleek coils, one over each ear. Choosing a new stage name – Molly Spotted Elk – she walked the maze of city sidewalks, knocking on the doors of agents and answering newspaper ads for dancers and models. She found work as a chorus girl and as a model for artists who found inspiration in her petite but powerful body and the fine elegance of her face.

By 1928 Molly Dellis had danced her way out of the chorus to win a solo spot in one of Texas Guinan's posh nightclubs. Throughout the Prohibition era Tex ran a string of sophisticated speakeasies, famous for dear prices and classy rebellious entertainment. The New York press heralded her as "the fairy disobedience, the patron of unruly children," and time and again headlined the "Hello Suckers!" greeting she used to welcome her guests. Police raided her clubs frequently on suspicion of liquor sales, but she had an uncanny knack for slipping through the hands of the law.

Tex showcased Molly Dellis as an exotic dancer, as did producers at other prestigious entertainment spots, including the Frivolity Night Club and the Shubert and Hollywood theaters. Often Molly accepted more than one job at a time and ran back and forth between two stages, doing six shows a night, working till dawn. Unfailingly, she sent part of her earnings home to her family, and whenever possible, she went home by train for a visit.

Of all the club owners and dance directors Molly Dellis worked for, none capitalized on her distinctly captivating style more than Texas Guinan. While Tex outfitted her other dancers with ostrich-feather fans, she featured Molly Spotted Elk in a floor-length eagle feather headdress – and little else. According to newspaper reviews, Molly "thrilled audiences."

For Molly Dellis, such responses were bittersweet. When she stepped onto the stage, she sometimes felt as if she stood before a cracked mirror held by demons. Tex required her showgirls to hobnob with customers between shows, and during these visits men in particular made it clear to Molly that they saw her as a "sexy savage," the embodiment of romantic dreams of ideal primitive life. Because the nightclub crowd applauded the fulfillment of such dreams over authenticity, Tex molded Molly into the cliché of an Indian princess. Molly found herself caught in a chasm between this imposed role and what she sensed within was right for herself. At times audience applause seemed like subtle guile, a means of making her into something she was not. She lived by it yet felt suspicious of it, afraid she would lose herself if she didn't resist this reward of trite artistry.

After shows Molly Dellis often found would-be suitors waiting for her – "stage-door Johnnies," she called them. Unsure of her social standing among these moneyed white men, she felt wary of their intentions and kept up her guard. This diary comment about one of her admirers is typical: "Wen at the club to see me. But his mother has higher hopes for her son – imagine her pride in love with a poor Indian girl. Wen is 'somebody's son' while I am merely nobody's daughter. His interest in me is mere fascination – a novelty to see if I am human."

At least one male patron who came to Texas Guinan's club saw Molly Dellis as more than a novelty. Douglas Burden, a dashing explorer-filmmaker and son of a millionaire, had spent the summers of his youth at his father's hunting camp in the remote forests of Quebec. As an adult he frequently ventured to far-off corners of the world to hunt wild animals for the American Museum of Natural History in New York City. This was the life he loved. Although educated by an elite corps of teachers at Groton and Harvard, he always said that his most influential tutor was his father's Ojibwe Indian hunting guide, who taught him a wealth of woods lore, camping skills, and hunting prowess. These early lessons made Burden cringe every time he saw one of Hollywood's standard film portrayals of Indians as wicked savages of the plains. In 1928 he decided to challenge this popularized image by producing a realistic docudrama of traditional Ojibwe life. He wrote the script himself and titled it *The Silent Enemy*. Beyond being a love story, it chronicled an Ojibwe band's struggle against starvation during winter months in northeast Canada. Burden needed a leading lady for his film, and he visited Tex's club expressly to see Molly's performance. After watching her dance and talking with her, he offered her the part. The script called for three leading men – a father, a lover, and an evil medicine man. Like Molly, the men chosen for these roles were formally schooled Native Americans who walked back and forth between Indian and white society.

After Molly Dellis and the other stars signed contracts with Burden, he spent six weeks canoeing along the shores of Abitibi Lake in northern Ontario to gather a supporting cast of more than one hundred "bush Indians," who still spent the winter months deep in the forest trapping fur-bearing animals. Then the entire cast and crew pitched camp in the heart of the Temagami Forest. They spent a year on location, accessible to the outside world only by canoe and dog sled. Aiming for an authentic re-creation of tribal life before European contact, Burden devoted the first month on location to filming the Ojibwes as they set up a traditional village – making wigwams, canoes, tools, snowshoes, toboggans, and skin clothing in the old ways.

For Molly Dellis, working on *The Silent Enemy* combined artistry, Native traditions, and the glories of nature in all its seasons. In her diary she wrote glowingly of camp life, including the simple pleasures of "sliding and snowshoeing in winter, swimming and fishing in the summer, and merry evenings of cards, dominoes, and singing." She took delight in the creative and intellectual companionship of Burden, the film crew, and her three male costars, as much as in the traditional wilderness savvy of the so-called bush Indians whom she referred to in her diary as "injuns."

For all its joys, the experience exposed some disturbing contradictions about Molly Dellis's social standing. The arrangement of the film camp's living quarters reflected the familiar pattern of racial segregation. The Ojibwes lived four-to-eight family members per tent. Their canvas shelters stood in a cluster about eighty feet away from the spacious two-person tents on platforms that housed the film's white executives and production crew, plus Molly Dellis and the Indian men with leading roles. Molly and these select neighbors dined in the cookery on food that was prepared for them, while the Ojibwes cooked for themselves and ate in their tents. Although Molly visited the Ojibwe encampment almost every day – usually to see an old fortune-teller who played the role of a medicine woman in the film – she spent most of her time with the film's white elite. More than any of them, she felt drawn to Burden and soon admitted to her diary that she had fallen in love with him. At first he returned her affections, but then, suddenly, he withdrew from her with no explanation. Molly found out why when she happened upon a note written by someone in Burden's circle, warning him to stay away from her: "Don't forget your reputation and what your friends would think. For you are human and that Indian girl is attractive. To think we eat at the same table with her!" Reading the words, Molly Dellis gasped, and her hand flew to her face as if to soothe a slap. Later, she wrote in her diary: "What am I? Only an Indian girl – with an illusion of love for someone far beyond me." Once again she felt lost in a social crack – this time in between the white and wealthy Burden and his batch of "bush Indians."

When the shoot ended, Molly Dellis left Canada and retreated to her own reservation where acceptance was assured and success or failure in the outside world counted for little. She stayed home long enough to restore her soul. Then she returned to New York, moved into a simple boarding house, and again took up club and theater work. In May 1930 *The Silent Enemy* debuted at Broadway's prestigious Criterion Theater. Without exception, critics lauded the film for its "authenticity," "stunning cinematography," and "superb acting," but it failed commercially. As a silent picture released amid a flurry of new "talkies," it did not stand a chance at the box office. For Molly, the long-term blessing of the movie was what it enabled her to do for her family: she used her substantial earnings to buy and furnish a house for them. The biggest abode on the reservation became their home – and her life-long retreat.

After a year in the wilderness, it did not take Molly Dellis long to grow sick of the hours, the repertoire, and the milieu of club work in a big city. More than ever she felt stifled by her audiences' views of "Indian maidens" and what she saw as the shallow attitudes of her dance directors. One of them was fond of saying that his dancers' costumes were *so tiny* that he had them flown in by humming birds. "My costume made me embarrassed," Molly told her diary – a loin cloth affair of satin and beads. "I'm just an injun in the flesh parade." In defiance of that narrow role, she began hauling her typewriter to dance engagements so she could write between shows. Sitting at her dressing table, she typed out some of the old Penobscot legends that Hemlock Joe had told her many years before.

Other American Indian performers shared her frustration. Many, including Molly Dellis, joined organizations such as the Aboriginal Council, which filed formal complaints about stage and film portrayals of Indians. Molly also joined the Society of the First Sons and Daughters of America, founded by Cherokee soprano Atalie Unkalunt to "provide authentic Amerinds with fine and dignified opportunities for artistic expression." The occasional concerts sponsored by the society challenged racial stereotypes but hardly erased them. Molly Dellis and her fellow Indian artists from New York to Hollywood continued struggling to find a balance between making a living and being true to themselves. As off-reservation Indians marketing themselves to mainstream society, they lived in a cultural no-man's land. Their sense of displacement matched that of "Hollywood Indians" written about in the *New York Herald Tribune*:

Hollywood has acquired a permanent colony of representatives of almost all tribes still existing. With the cinema as their melting pot, these expatriates are taking on the semblance of a tribe all their own. One among them has taken the initiative of applying to the Bureau of Indian Affairs for recognition of the "De Mille Indians" as a new tribe composed only of Indians who work in films. A Hollywood tribe is not beyond the imagination; for most of us the only real Indian is a Hollywood Indian.

For Molly Dellis and other Native American performers, the "real Indian" was not the one they presented on stage or in front of a camera. It was the inner self of each of them, tied to the freeborn lifeways of their forebears and waiting to be articulated. It was the true self that Molly longed to grasp and express through her work. Instead, she found herself half-naked on a stage, doing dances that only hinted at the depth of her being. One day she made this diary entry: "How I wish I could have the proper atmosphere to do my work as it should be. The more I dance, the more I want to interpret my emotions without limitation, to create a freedom of primitiveness and abandon. If only one could dance solely for art! Maybe someday I will have that chance. If not in America, then in Europe."

Molly's wish came true in 1931. She traveled to France with the famous United States Indian Band and performed the opening dance for the International Colonial Exposition in Paris. Back home her family listened to a broadcast of the event on a radio she had bought for her mother several years earlier – the first radio on Indian Island. Appearing daily with the Indian Band at the American exhibit, Molly received a lot of press coverage and numerous invitations for other engagements. The first time she performed at the chic Ritz Hotel, her audience shouted "Bis! Bis!" Always prepared for jeering, Molly Dellis thought they were calling her a *beast*. In fact, they were calling for an encore. She decided to give them a big one. When the band returned to the United States after several months, Molly stayed behind, drawn by French audiences which seemed less racist and more sophisticated than those at home. As one French journalist reported at the time: "Princess Spotted Elk is emphatic in her desire for nothing but genuineness and she tells of the struggle she had in the States for a true appreciation of Indian dances. 'The average American,' the princess declares, 'is satisfied with a dancer bedecked in feathers, making war-whoops and leaping aimlessly about with savage gestures to the beat of a tom-tom.' "

Over the next few years, Molly Dellis basked in the admiration she found abroad. She danced throughout Europe for an array of audiences, including royalty. She also lectured professionally on In-dian cultures, including dance – sometimes giving a combination lecture and dance as she had done while attending the University of Pennsylvania. She continued writing down the legends she had learned as a child, even began work on a novel about nineteenth-century life on Indian Island, and mingled in Parisian cafes with artists, writers, and anthropologists.

Molly Dellis's most frequent and intimate French companion was Jean Archambaud, a journalist with *Paris Soir,* the city's leading daily newspaper. As a special correspondent, Jean spent much time outside the office, gathering material for a wide variety of feature stories. His wide-ranging interests included anthropology, natural history, philosophy, and the arts, so it was not surprising that he requested an interview with the beautiful American Indian dancer soon after her arrival in Paris. Sitting with her at a sidewalk cafe, he asked what she thought of his fair city. "It is too loud," she answered. "I prefer the woods." Not all Parisians would have appreciated this response, but Jean Archambaud found it enchanting.

Over the next few weeks, during lingering talks in cafes and long strolls through Parisian parks, Jean discovered that Molly Dellis relished art, literature, and history as much as he did and that she too felt uneasy if she spent too much time away from nature. She spoke with a captivating blend of passion and knowledge about a tribal culture that fascinated him. She sang Penobscot songs to him and told him the old Indian legends. He pursued her as a reflection of something deep within himself. Within a month he wrote his first love letter to her:

At last it seems to me I have reached all that I have craved for. You opened the door and here in the entrance I stand, marveling. It is all I wanted and more. I want to pray and kneel, and at the same moment I could jump and give some joy whoop.

You are the guide, a delicious guide for my clumsy footsteps. You take me by the arm and show me the path. And the road is lovely, splendid. I bathe in an ether so beautiful. I breathe it and my heart is filled with awe and love. Your language is poetic and musical. And far back, years and years, it seems familiar. I feel that the life of the "Old Time" must have been mine too. The simple songs you sang to me pleased me more than I will be able to tell you. In them there is a reflection of rushing water, wind in treetops, and blazing campfires.

And there our souls were united and flew like two colorful birds into the trees. Thousands of tiny musicians played for us, but none could be

*seen. It was the music of the Red gods and I was united to you in the
simple and sacred ways of your people – of my people.*
I can hardly write. It is impossible to express all that is in my heart.

Two weeks later Jean proposed marriage. Despite the undeniable
pull he had on Molly Dellis, she held back, afraid to surrender her
heart and certain that any formal union would kill her career. She had
always given priority to her profession: "The fire of ambition must
be first," she had told her diary at age twenty-three.

By autumn, however, Molly began to have a change of heart. It
happened while she and Jean were hiking in the Pyrenees in southern
France. As Molly climbed the steep flank of a mountain, her eyes were
on the summit but her thoughts were on the tempting man walking
just behind her. The rhythm of Jean's sure footsteps and the slight
heaving of his breath filled the space between them. His presence
pulled at her thoughts, weighting her steps with unbearable pleasure.
The slope became the angle of his cheek. The crest became his brow.
Her feet were hands, and every stride a caress. Upon reaching the
brow, she turned to him and said, "I have a story to tell you."

They sat on a lip of the mountain, facing the Atlantic Ocean. At
their backs rose the great spine of the Pyrenees, dividing France from
Spain. Well below them crouched the fishing village of St. Jean de
Luz. As the setting sun lit up the sea and the sky and Molly Dellis's
face, she closed her eyes, slipped back in time, and began.

"Three centuries ago, a young nobleman left these shores and
sailed across the ocean to the land of my ancestors. His name was
Jean Vincent d'Abbadie, and his father was the baron of a place called
St. Castin, not far from here. Jean Vincent was a boy soldier – just
thirteen years old – and King Louis XIV had given his regiment a
charge that must have thrilled a youngster eager for adventure. They
were to do battle against the fearsome Iroquois who were raiding
Wabanaki villages and attacking the settlements of our French allies
near Quebec. After defeating the Iroquois, Jean Vincent's regiment
disbanded. Several years later he found his way to the homeland of
my people and chose to stay there and live with them. He was a good
trader and always paid Indian trappers well for their furs. For decades
he fought side by side with my ancestors against the English who were

stealing our land. He became the Baron of St. Castin after the death of his father and older brother, but even that did not lure him away from my people. He became friends with one of our most famous chiefs, Madockawando, and married his beautiful daughter, Molly Mathilde. People called her the Indian baroness. When she gave birth to Jean Vincent's children, his bond with Penobscots grew even stronger and my people honored him as a chief."

Molly Dellis opened her eyes and turned to Jean, whose gaze had never left her face. "And that is how a Frenchman became an Indian chief, a husband to an Indian woman, and father to a family of French-Indian children," she told him with a smile. "I've always had the feeling that my family stemmed from the marriage of St. Castin and Molly Mathilde," she added.

"Perhaps you and I are related," said Jean, placing his palms on her cheeks. Then he looked at her so lovingly that her own eyes grew tender. "Shall we write about St. Castin and Molly Mathilde one day?" he asked, wrapping his arms around Molly Dellis and pressing his temple to hers. *Yes,* she thought. Then they watched the horizon in silence until the sun disappeared and night made them one.

After their mountain trek Molly Dellis knew absolutely that Jean Archambaud was not like other white suitors who had pursued her. She recognized him as a kindred spirit and told this to her diary: "At times, I would swear Jean had injun feeling – for he understands so well. As it is, the arms of the forest enveloped him in his childhood, and its warmth and mysteries saturated his white skin and soul."

Nonetheless, the thought of marriage made Molly uneasy. Confronted with a love as strong as her ambition, she wrote: "Sooner or later, I, as a woman, will have to make a choice between two things. I will be happy in my work and lonely, or happy with someone and discontented with my work and myself."

Eventually, her fears about the limitations of marriage would be overcome by what she described as the "companionship, honesty, honor, understanding, and confidence" that she found with Jean. But for the time being they lived together as lovers.

An intimate relationship of deep tenderness and true friendship grew between the Penobscot dancer and the French writer. Both traveled often for their work, she performing, he researching articles.

Whenever possible, they traveled and worked together. Equally drawn to nature, the two of them sometimes hiked dozens of miles through the countryside toward Molly's next engagement. Once there, she would step out of her boots, into her dance moccasins, and onto the stage, and he would hop a train to his next assignment. Back in Paris they coauthored newspaper and magazine stories about their treks and about American Indian topics. Jean supported Molly's career enthusiastically, translating her public lectures, painting costumes for her, and sometimes even donning Indian garb himself to play the drum while she danced.

In France, Molly Dellis's dancing matured. One critic described her as "an exquisite artist whose movements are extraordinary, practically non-human." In Paris, her work won her a select place as a performing artist in the Cercle Internationale des Arts, which sponsored recitals for the city's leading arts patrons and critics. Weary and wary of dance halls, she welcomed such sophisticated audiences. Dancing for them, she found modest fame and respect, and to her this was sweet success.

The sweetness did not last. By spring 1933 the Great Depression had cast its pall over Europe, and France stood on the brink of devastating economic and political strife. Molly Dellis's opportunities to perform plummeted, as did her paychecks, and Jean lost his job because of partisan politics and major cutbacks in the newspaper industry. Reduced to freelancing, he sold articles when and where he could, often for a pittance. At the same time, Molly became ill, suffering for months with chronic flu and painful boils, which made it all but impossible for her to dance.

Molly and Jean had never been financially well off, but now they could barely pay their rent and at times did not even have money for food. "I'm just helpless," Molly told her diary. "My health is shot to pieces. Blood comes from me every day. I'm undernourished. No work. It's all so discouraging."

Then, early in 1934, Molly Dellis found that she was pregnant. This was unwelcome news. Coming on top of her other challenges, it stirred a homesickness in her that she had held under control but never fully conquered. Now she wrote about it almost daily in her diary:

With injuns again in my imagination. Have been terribly homesick, tired of civilization, white people and the city.

If I could only be back home in the woods to fill my eye, heart, mind and lungs with just pure air, trees and contentment – and in the mystery of nature find inspiration.

Watched the sky for a long time. Oh god, to be back in the wilderness. Am so tired of noises and white people – everyone but Jean.

Oh, to hear injun voices speak and the sound of someone pounding an ash log somewhere in the distance.

Finally, she could endure the yearning no longer. After talking it over with Jean, she decided to return home long enough to have their child and recover her health. A friend helped by giving her money to buy a ticket on a trans-Atlantic freight ship. Molly and Jean tried to get married before her departure, only to find she lacked the necessary papers.

On Molly's last night in Paris, the skies wept. The next morning she wrote a short entry in her diary: "Rainy. Packed all night with J. Had to sleep an hour or so – In his arms." Among the items packed was a Cree Indian cradleboard that Jean had bought for their baby from a local collector. Molly, in turn, had something for Jean: a Penobscot name. She chose Neebowset, which means "Night Walker," a name for the moon. Later, when the distance between them seemed unbearable, she would look for Neebowset in the night sky and find consolation.

The day after landing in the United States Molly Dellis gave birth to a daughter, whom she named Jean, after her lover. To avoid confusion, she began calling Jean Archambaud "Johnny." Molly had never wanted to be a mother, but with little Jean came a fulfillment she had never imagined, a primal bond with the child and her father – with Life itself.

When her baby was seven months old, Molly Dellis reluctantly left the girl in her mother's care on Indian Island and returned to New York where she hoped to earn enough money for both of them to return to Paris. It proved to be a sorry struggle. The depression wore on, her old employer Texas Guinan had died, and Molly remained physically worn from her illness and pregnancy. She did find some club work, small parts in big films, and a bit of modeling work, but she earned barely enough to support herself and send money home for her daughter, let alone pay for the expensive boat trip back to France. Even if the money had come swiftly and easily, Molly could not have traveled freely, for she felt anxious about taking her child to a distant land where political turmoil and uncertainty were on the rise.

Throughout their separation Molly Dellis and Johnny wrote each other often and even managed to collaborate on a few articles for French publications. On his own, Archambaud penned controversial political commentaries and began in-depth research for a book comparing navies of the world, while Molly finally finished writing down all the Penobscot legends that old Hemlock Joe had told her so long ago. In libraries and archives on either side of the ocean both of them began researching the story that echoed their own – the seventeenth-century love affair between Molly Mathilde of the Penobscot River valley and Jean Vincent of St. Castin.

Ultimately, it was this absorbing story that compelled Molly Dellis to return to France with her daughter to reunite with Johnny, regardless of the risks. After discovering that circumstances of politics and war had forever cut Molly Mathilde from St. Castin, Molly Dellis had resolved that this would not happen to her and Johnny.

When Jean Archambaud met Molly Dellis at the harbor and swept his four-year-old daughter into his arms for the first time, Molly knew she had made the right decision. In the months that followed, she only grew more convinced that it was right and good that she had returned, no matter what lay ahead. Their finances remained precarious, and the brutal Nazi regime in neighboring Germany threatened the entire continent, but she and Johnny finally married, and little Jean came to know her father and to garner a treasure trove of stories about him and about their life together as a family in his land.

Molly Dellis had few dance engagements during this second stay in France. Instead, she tended to her child and collaborated with Johnny on various freelance articles. Periodically, she worked on her profile about the Indian doctress Molly Ockett, finding inspiration in this foremother's bold and creative responses to the predicaments of her life.

In the summer of 1939 something wonderful happened. After putting the finishing touches on her collection of Wabanaki legends, Molly Dellis found a French publisher. But on the first day of September, just before the promotional campaign for the book was to begin, German troops invaded Poland. Two days later, in response to this aggression, France and England declared war on Germany, and Molly's long-cherished stories became one of the casualties of war.

Soon thereafter, out of money and running low on hope, Molly Dellis and her husband left Paris and with their daughter moved southwest to Royan, where Johnny's parents lived. Long associated with the Boy Scouts, Archambaud found a job as Regional Scout Master there. With the help of his teenage charges, he managed the city's growing war refugee center, tending the needs of people uprooted from Germany, Austria, Poland, and Czechoslovakia – most of them Jews. In time, as the war escalated and the battles came closer to home, they would also assist the Red Cross in caring for wounded soldiers from the front. The job provided Archambaud with food and a two-room cottage for his family, but no salary.

With each passing month, the work grew more demanding. By May, long grueling hours at the center left Archambaud little time with his wife and daughter. While he minded the needs of refugees and injured soldiers, Molly Dellis took care of their child, sheltering her as much as possible from the tragedy unfolding around them. When Johnny's absence overlapped with Jean's afternoon nap or nighttime sleep, Molly worked on her manuscript about Molly Ockett, marveling at the woman's resilience and strength, feeling guilty that she could not always call up these qualities in her own life. Archambaud, overworked by the escalating miseries of war, often labored around the clock. Day after day he did not make it home for dinner, let alone for a full night's sleep beside his wife. Consumed by the urgent needs of so many victims, he had little time or energy to consider the plight of his own family. This deepened Molly's worry over what would become of them. Her response to his absence sometimes erupted as jealous despair. One lonely night, in the furious whisper of her minuscule handwriting, she told her diary: "Jean's ear bothered her but that did not concern her father so much as the refugees, Scouts or this or that meeting. He said that a train of refugees were coming in and it was necessary that he be there to meet it, to which I answered that he should have the same responsibility about his family as he has for them." Yet when Johnny came home at dawn and drew Molly close to him in their bed, her anger dissolved in his embrace.

Molly Dellis's main focus during this time was securing the papers necessary for her family to travel to America together. Repeatedly, the U. S. Consulate denied Archambaud a visa. When Molly pressed for an explanation, officials told her that he had a heart condition that would make him incapable of earning a living in the United States. Neither she nor Johnny believed what they were told. More likely the denial stemmed from the highly charged political articles he wrote and a suspicion – brought on by his extensive investigation of world navies – that he had served in the French secret service.

In early June, France surrendered Paris to Germany, and Hitler's heavily armed legions filed in and took charge of the capital. Anticipating their arrival, four-fifths of the city's five million citizens had already fled, including government officials. A week later, French authorities signed an armistice with Germany, choosing a middle ground between total capitulation and a prolonged battle for which the nation lacked both the will and resources. Terms of the truce forced French taxpayers to finance German occupation and control of more than half of their country – all territory north of Vichy, plus a broad strip along the entire Atlantic Coast.

By the time both sides signed the agreement, German troops were already en route to take possession of the coast, including Royan. French soldiers based in the city hastily prepared to leave, since those who stayed behind were likely to be taken as prisoners of war. Archambaud, as a journalist known for political articles and naval research, also faced the possibility of arrest. He was at danger on another score as well. As an able-bodied man whose job with refugees would end under German occupation, he could be rounded up and forced to work in a German labor camp – along with the Scouts who had been entrusted to his care. Backed into a corner, he realized that his only choice now was to lead the Scouts out of the immediate danger zone. He yearned to take his wife and child with him, but the only feasible escape plan was far too risky. They would be safer traveling on their own. So, just hours before the Germans arrived, Molly kissed her beloved husband good-bye, and he and his young men slipped away from Royan in a boat headed up the Gironde River. Under the veil of darkness they traveled southeast toward unoccupied French territory, having no idea where they would ultimately find shelter.

The morning after Johnny's sudden departure, Molly Dellis opened her diary and wrote: "After a sleepless night haunted by thoughts, tears, memories, and by the vivid face of J with tears in his eyes, I felt desperately alone with Jean. To be alone with her at this time under these circumstances has been a hard blow. I feel mechanical. It is as if all of my being were numbed to lethargy. Part of myself is gone, abruptly, broken by the cruel hands of circumstances."

When the German troops and tanks descended upon Royan, the numbness broke, and Molly Dellis told her diary: "Panic ahead, wonder, doubt, prayers, longing, writing – and a woman walks alone. Everywhere there are Germans. There remains only one thing for me: to go home with Jean."

Like so many refugees on the run, Molly Dellis and her little girl headed south for the Spanish border. She managed to secure a ride as far as Bordeaux, and from there she and the six-year-old continued on foot, often under the shadows of German war planes. With a suitcase in one hand and her daughter's hand in the other, Molly trudged through fields, hitched short rides, slept along the roadside. At times she practically carried the child. Finally, relying on her strong dancer's legs, she got them over the Pyrenees Mountains into Spain. In Bilbao they found a train to Lisbon, Portugal. A day later, they arrived at the port city with barely enough time to book passage on a refugee steamer that would take them back to America, so far from Johnny. On board, while others slept, Molly paced the deck deep into the night, her face tilted upward, her eyes fixed on the light of Neebowset, the Night Walker.

As always, Indian Island provided a refuge. This time Molly Dellis did not leave the reservation to seek work in New York. Instead, she tended the vegetable garden, braided sweetgrass for baskets, worked on the tribal census committee, helped initiate a local civil defense unit, and waited for word from her husband. At last, as summer drew to a close, a letter arrived. Molly's mother brought it to her in the kitchen where she was trimming beans. Knife in hand, Molly sat down at the table and slit open the envelope. Heart racing, she scanned the letter swiftly. Then, she turned to her mother and whispered, "He's all right."

After a long and arduous journey, Archambaud and the Scouts had made it safely to southern France. As Molly reread his letter, sitting outside by the river, she realized that he had written her from Pau – the city where St. Castin had spent his final years! For just a moment, her thoughts ran back in time, and she imagined Molly Mathilde waiting on this very island for her husband to disentangle himself from Pau and come to her. Recalling that Molly Mathilde's waiting had been in vain, Molly Dellis broke this train of thought and refocused on the pleasure of picturing Johnny safe beyond German lines. In his next letter, he told her that he and the Scouts had moved on after hearing rumors that the Germans might come to Pau. Finally, they settled at a secure refugee camp and medical center near Toulouse. There, they cared for, cooked for, and tried to cheer some three hundred wounded soldiers and refugees. "We earn our food this way," he wrote. "Sometimes we play Indian theatres for them and I beat the tom-tom and think of you."

During the next year, Molly and Johnny wrote countless pages to each other, numbering their letters in hope of knowing which ones had made it through the broken mail service of wartime. With each passing month, Archambaud's letters grew increasingly desperate as his hopes of getting a U. S. visa faded and his health deteriorated. On 24 September 1941 he wrote: "This life is breaking. My health is not so good. . . . I am too weak to walk much . . . but by hook or crook I will reach you." He never did. He died the following month. The awful news came to Molly Dellis in a letter from a friend of his who wrote that Archambaud had suffered from heart disease and passed away "with your name on his lips, Madame."

The unspeakable sadness that engulfed Molly Dellis after her husband's death soon transformed into rage over life's cruelty. She fed her fury by digging into the life of Molly Molasses, known as the bitterest and most forceful Penobscot woman of all time. Molly Dellis hoped anger would strengthen her, but it did nothing of the kind. It made her soul hard and cold, and she felt herself moving numbly through life, as if her veins were frozen streams.

Before winter set in, the United States entered the war. Unmoved by the growing drama, Molly Dellis watched her brothers and many other Penobscot men leave home to join the army. Unable to feel anything, Molly wanted to be alone. One cold, dreary day she wandered back to New York, leaving her daughter in Philomene's care. The city had little to offer an Indian dancer these days, especially an aging woman who had lost her radiance. She lived in tiny rooms and found odd jobs – as a worker in a shoe factory, a waitress in a coffee shop, a YMCA mail clerk. She held this last job for some time. Soon after the war ended – and five years after Archambaud's death – she began to open up to another man's kindness. He was an American soldier who stayed at the YMCA whenever he had a weekend leave in the city. Slowly, he melted the icy veins leading to Molly Dellis's heart. He talked to her at the mail counter, took her out for coffee, then dinner. He bought her simple gifts, which she accepted as treasures. But he did not tell her about his wife and children. In 1948, when the army transferred him to California, he abruptly cut off all communication with Molly.

She could not bear another loss. Again, her veins turned to ice. This time so swiftly that she snapped.

Molly Dellis spent a year in the Bangor State Mental Institute before surrendering her bitterness. Finally, late in the summer of 1949, something within her turned, and she found her way back home to Indian Island, where she began to look anew at her own life. Reading her old diaries, she sought sweetness among the sorrows. In those pages, she found Hemlock Joe telling the old legends. There was Professor Speck, writing down the tales and teaching her to do the same. She rediscovered the smells, sights, and sounds of the woods on Indian Island. She saw herself strolling with her father under the stars and calling them by name. She glimpsed her mother's artful hands young again, weaving baskets. With fresh eyes, she saw her passion for dance, and she relived falling in love with a Frenchman and giving birth to their daughter.

Then, inexplicably, she stopped.

Telling her mother and teenage daughter that she had to leave the island again to find work, Molly Dellis returned to the bustle of New York City. This time, almost no one would hire her, and whenever she found a job it did not last long. Often she roamed the crowded sidewalks aimlessly, with no place to stay, nowhere to go. For weeks on end she felt hungry and sick. In 1951 a Broadway journalist who had written about her often in her days of glory wrote this in his column: "It has come to my attention that Molly Spotted Elk, once a famous dancer who got her start with Texas Guinan, is desperately ill and penniless. Surely this genuine American girl – whose forefathers were famed Indian chiefs, occupying American soil long before Columbus spotted the precious land – cannot be abandoned at this time."

His words brought no help, and another year passed without relief for Molly. Then, deeply troubled about her dismal situation, eighteen-year-old Jean sent her mother a letter, begging her to leave New York: "I thought of you so much on Christmas Eve. I cried because I didn't know whether or not you even had a place to stay. It is hell worrying about you out there. Not sure you have enough to eat, any money, whether you are warm. Mommie, why don't you come home? Please Mommie, don't be stubborn and foolish. I'll help you."

At last, once and for all, Molly Dellis went home. In her absence a new one-lane bridge had replaced the ferry that had long linked Indian Island to Old Town. Now it was quicker and safer to travel between the reservation and the mainland. To Molly, the bridge signaled the end of an era, a moment in time when most Penobscots had finally given in to the ways of the white world. All of her brothers and sisters had left the island by way of that bridge and never looked back. Nearly everyone on the reservation called it progress, but her father Horace called it "paradise lost." Still, with or without the bridge, Indian Island remained a haven for Molly, a place where the trees still stood and the river still flowed.

Shortly after Molly Dellis's return, her daughter Jean married and moved away, and Molly shared the house with only her father and mother. Serenity was still not hers, but she could see it there in the distance, and she tried to live life in a way that kept it within sight. She spent her days quietly – reading, writing, keeping the garden, walking in the woods, and making Indian dolls and baskets. In time, her daughter Jean had a son and a daughter of her own, and sometimes she brought them to Indian Island for a visit. When they came, Molly Dellis relived the sweet parts of her own childhood and invited her grandchildren into a magical realm where ancient stories came to life, everything in the forest had a name, and where one might catch a fish by hand.

In 1962 Molly Dellis's father, Horace, died. Whenever Molly missed his company, she would stroll down to the great river, because that was the place she could best feel his presence. Occasionally, she took along one of her old diaries. After some hours of quiet reading and reflection, she would walk back home, sit down before the old typewriter, and add a bit to the story of her life. One March day in 1969, just before winter gave way to spring, she climbed into her boots, wrapped herself in a long coat and shawl, and turned down the forest path that led to the place by the river where Hemlock Joe's shack once stood. Reaching the water's edge, she snapped several boughs from an evergreen and made a seat for herself atop the snowy bank. Sitting there, back propped against the sturdy trunk, she randomly opened her 1929 diary. Her eyes fell upon an entry made on 20 March, exactly forty years earlier when she was just twenty-five: "The beautiful things live on and heal the wounds of sorrow," it said. Closing her eyes, Molly Dellis held to this precious thought, and like the river on a hot summer day, it beckoned her. She dove in and it embraced her. Then she drank it in and swallowed its joy.

After some time, a cool breeze brushed Molly's cheek. She opened her eyes and gazed at the frozen stillness of the snow-clad river. She imagined the river continuing to flow below its icy surface. How often she had sat in this very spot on warmer days and watched it travel, marveling at how it ran its course with determination, ever moving, yet never gone. Throughout her life she had longed to be like the river, to cut deeply and run undaunted in one broad bed, connecting the traditions of her people to her wider world in a timeless unity, gathering up the worthy parts of all ages and peoples. And she longed to overcome obstacles as the river did: when it came upon an obstruction such as a beaver dam, it waited and widened, building volume until it outgrew the barrier, hurled itself over the top, and continued on its way.

Suddenly, something just upstream caught Molly's eye. Someone was walking on the snow-covered ice. She squinted to bring the figure into focus. No, there were *three* people. Three women silhouetted against the snowscape in the late afternoon sun. She watched them make their way downstream in her direction. They were dressed alike, each wearing a traditional peaked cap and clutching a heavy blanket around her shoulders. But each had a distinct way of walking. One moved with fluid grace, one with long strong strides, and one had a rather fitful but stalwart gait. As they passed by, leaving footprints in the river, she knew they were her three Mollies. They were talking with one another, and she could just make out some of their words: "Nothing done for love is wasted. . . . It enlarges the heart. . . . On the strength of such feelings, we go on." At that moment, Molly Dellis saw that these Wabanaki foremothers were her examples of true strength after all. They were her spirit guides. They may not have defined their circumstances, but they fought against being defined by them. Although they were robbed of much that was dear, they never surrendered their dignity, their moral centers, their souls. There was, after all, something that could not be taken – spiritual freedom, the freedom to choose one's attitude in any situation.

Molly Dellis held the trio in her gaze until they disappeared in the distance. Then she scanned the length of the trail they had left. Soon, their firm footprints would melt in the early spring sun and become part of a river that would leave something green in its wake.

And what about her? What would she leave in her wake? This was all she knew: from the time she was a girl she had tried to preserve and foster respect for traditional culture by giving it to the public in dance, song, lecture, and writing. The first stage name she chose for herself had been Neeburban, the Penobscot word for Northern Lights. The name reflected the light or insight she yearned for and wanted to share with others through her art. She had told her diary, "With hard work I will achieve my goal – not fame but realization."

What had she realized? As a mother, a wife, and a dancer, she had glimpsed the power of genuine love and pure art. They had, indeed, enlarged her heart and strengthened her in her life's journey. She was beginning to see that each life is but part of the River of Life, that someone always follows to carry on what others have started, that the beautiful in life really does remain to heal the wounds of sorrow.

Molly Dellis stood, stepped carefully down the bank onto the frozen river, and followed the trail of her foremothers. After walking some distance, she looked back to see if she had left any footprints of her own.

Some years later, in the full green of a spring day, Molly Dellis sat in a chair under the apple tree in her yard. The tree grew near the house, which stood on a knoll. Looking down the slope to her left, Molly could see the river and to her right the graveyard. It had been an interesting week. Two young Penobscot women had come by to ask her about the old days. They wanted information about the past, they said, because they needed it to build a better future. They spoke of Red Power and of getting back land stolen from Penobscots years ago. They had plans, ambitions. Molly began to tell them about the days long before the bridge, about her foremothers, about Hemlock Joe's stories, and about snake dances and waltzes in the old tribal hall. They did not stay long, but when they left, they said they would return. And now, still thinking of them, Molly had come outside with her 1925 diary, written when she was about their age. Sitting there under the pale pink blossoms in the late afternoon, she started to open her diary, only to be distracted by the trill of a woodcock somewhere near the river. Looking up, she spotted the bird in flight – his plump russet body, round gray head, long bill, and ridiculous little tail – spiraling higher and higher into the lavender sky until he passed out of sight. Moments later, he reappeared, tumbling wildly toward the earth as if he had been shot. But seconds before hitting the ground, his wings suddenly flared open, and the fellow righted himself and landed squarely on his feet in a glade alongside the river. With barely a pause, he took wing again and repeated his entire aerial mating dance. When he finished his performance, Molly called out spontaneously, "I, too, danced for life!" After watching him a bit longer, she returned to her diary. Opening the book, she read a passage written when she was twenty-three. "The fire of ambition must be first," it said. She laughed at her younger self. *Not ambition*, she thought, *but love – of family, tradition, and the dance of Life.*

PORTAGE

The goal in any portage is to reunite with the river.

21 February 1977: Indian Island, Old Town, Maine

The years passed, and Molly Dellis's story remained unfinished. With the death of her mother, Molly now lived alone in the house she had bought for her family nearly fifty years earlier. In the first hours of a thawed winter's morning, the river's thick ice sheet creaked and groaned and stirred Molly from her sleep. Opening her eyes, she saw moon shadows dancing on the walls. For a long while she lay still, watching the dance and listening to the river sing of the Sowing Moon's approach. Then she climbed out of bed, pulled on her robe, and walked through the empty house, fondly recalling its fullness. Coming to the top of the back stairway that led down to the kitchen, she paused at a small window and looked out at the full moon. It glowed so brightly that Molly could almost feel its light shining warm on her face. For a moment, reflected in the glass, she saw her face at one with the moon. "Neebowset," she whispered tenderly. As she turned to go downstairs for a drink of water, she tripped and fell to the bottom of the stairs. Within the house, all became still, while outside, the moonlight revealed Molly Dellis's footprints in the river.

METHODOLOGY & REFERENCES

Women of the Dawn is an interpretation of Wabanaki Indian history grounded in historical and ethnographic documentation. Working on it, I had the benefit of personal ties to Wabanaki tribal communities in Maine and the Canadian Maritimes. The writing has been guided by insights gained from the private papers of Molly Dellis Nelson Archambaud, as well as numerous interviews with living Penobscots and other Wabanakis, conducted since 1981. Two Penobscot women read and commented on this book while it was still in manuscript form – Molly Dellis's daughter, Jean Archambaud Moore, and Donna Loring, the tribe's representative to the Maine State Legislature.

I cannot overemphasize the value of consulting the present-day descendants of the people one writes about from the past. I first encountered the wealth of information and historical insight held in the hearts and minds of Wabanaki Indians while working on the oral histories of Micmac women elders in the early 1980s. Because their life stories were gathered for the federal recognition and land claims effort of the Aroostook Band of Micmacs, they were never published. Working on them, however, greatly influenced my subsequent published work. It taught me the importance of writing in a way that not only advances scholarship, but also touches the people about whom one is writing. And it showed me that Native American women have played critical roles in assuring the economic, social, religious, and political well-being and survival of their tribes, despite their repeated absence in the written record. In the past decade some of my work has been devoted to unearthing and writing about their existence and influence in history. It includes a full-length biography about Molly Dellis, titled *Molly Spotted Elk: A Penobscot in Paris* (University of Oklahoma Press, 1995), as well as book chapters about two other Wabanaki women: "Walking the Medicine Line: Molly Ockett, a Pigwacket Doctor" (with Harald Prins), in *Northeastern Indian Lives 1632–1816*, edited by Robert Grumet (University of Massachusetts Press, 1996) and "Princess Watahwaso: Bright Star of the Penobscot," in *Thriving Beyond Expectations: Women in Maine 1850–1969*, edited by Polly Kaufman (University of Maine, 1999).

I have written *Women of the Dawn* from the standpoint that beyond ethnic distinctions, we all share a collective human heritage that enables us to widen our spheres of cultural empathy. All four women in this book came to terms with cultural otherness, and two of them transcended it through intimate relationships. Clearly it is possible to reach across cultural divides, to communicate with and understand one another, to glean insights from the experiences and perspectives of others. That said, it is important to note that I ventured into the lives of these women with caution and with deep respect for their particular ethnic identities, knowing that when one steps out of one's culture and time, what appears to be familiar may not be at all. When I started the book I was not really any closer to or farther away from St. Castin with whom I share "whiteness" than to Molly Mathilde with whom I share "womanhood." For this reason, the comments, attitudes, and insights of contemporary Penobscot women were of value to me as were those of my own European husband. Also aware that written records of the past are culturally and historically mediated, I have tried to bring a critical reading to the documentary references that provided the backbone for this book. In the end, *Women of the Dawn* is as faithful a historical retelling as I am able to write.

A few words are in order concerning my writing strategy as pertains to women's history. The fact that Molly Dellis kept research notes on Molly Mathilde gave birth to the book's unusual structure, including the idea to present all four profiles as if she wrote them. Assuming someone else's voice is a bold choice, but I have carried the idea to completion for several reasons. To begin with, presenting Wabanaki women's history as a personal quest for insight helps bring that history to life and makes it accessible to a wide readership. Also, I have become familiar with Molly Dellis's voice. I read all (and transcribed much) of her surviving diaries and correspondence during the two years I spent working on her full-length biography. Perhaps most important, I am convinced that Molly Dellis would have welcomed this effort to complete and build upon something she started. Although she did not get very far in her research for Molly Mathilde's story, she left clear traces of intent. Intrigued by those traces, I set out on a new research and writing journey of my own, the result of which is the book in hand. Although I do not claim that this is the book Molly Dellis would have written, her daughter, Jean Archambaud Moore, tells me that it is a book that speaks of her mother's yearning. Jean also appreciated the narrative strategy of using her mother's voice to tell the life stories of the "four Mollies."

Surviving remnants of Molly Dellis's research on Molly Mathilde consist of references to the effort in letters between Molly Dellis and her husband Jean Archambaud, as well as eighteen pages of research notes. She did this research in the 1930s at the University of Maine, Orono, Library, the New York Public Library, and the National Library in Paris. Molly was not a trained scholar, and she investigated the lives of Molly Mathilde and St. Castin at a time when ethnohistorical and ethnographic literature about the Wabanakis was rare and not easily accessible. Even Frank Speck's Classic *Penobscot Man* had not yet been published. However, Molly brought to her research a keen appreciation of history and a personal hunger for any wisdom it might hold relative to her own life. She also had a working understanding of French, as well as the ability to at least understand elders on the reservation who still spoke Penobscot or Maliseet. Most of her research notes are fragmented historical transcriptions having to do with French-Indian relations during the late seventeenth and early eighteenth centuries. They draw from reliable sources as well as from material such as Longfellow's legendary poetic portrayal of Molly Mathilde and St. Castin.

I did not rely on Molly Dellis's notes for scholarly purposes, but they provided essential evidence of her search – a compelling picture of a young Indian woman, delving into the past with the hope of gaining insight into her own life. It is noteworthy that Molly's personal papers include other historical explorations on Wabanaki life – from legends to herbal medicines to traditional dances. Some of these were done in preparation for the public talks she gave. For me, their value, like her notes on Molly Mathilde, was not scholarly, but psychological, revealing her love of and need for historical grounding.

Originally, I planned to write conventional ethnohistorical accounts of the four Mollies. I completed such a profile of Molly Mathilde. Given the dearth of specific information about her in the historical record, the early profile was impersonal and filled with academic qualifiers such as "she may have" and "it appears likely that," and so forth. Moreover, Molly Mathilde was eclipsed by the historical events and by the better-chronicled male characters who surrounded her, including her illustrious father, husband, and son. When I read through the finished piece, it felt out of balance and left me cold. I asked my husband, an ethnohistorian, to take a look. His comment was, "This woman doesn't *breathe*." He was right. I knew I would encounter similar problems with Molly Molasses and, to a lesser extent with Molly Ockett (all in contrast to Molly Dellis, whose twentieth-century life left a less obscure trail).

With this in mind, I decided to try my hand at creative nonfiction with Molly Dellis as the book's narrator. I filled some of the holes in the other women's lives with reconstructed scenes firmly tethered to the historical and ethnographically informed record. For example, although the record tells us that Molly Mathilde's son died at age nine in his first year of school in Quebec, it reveals nothing of Molly's reaction to his death. How to convey this sad event in its fullness? How to relay both the fact *and* the feeling of misfortune? My reconstruction is based on the sorrow that this loss would bring to any mother, combined with the fact that Molly Mathilde was a Christian convert, steeped in traditional Wabanaki mourning rituals. These rituals, as described in historical records, included the blackening of one's face with soot and bear grease. So I pictured Molly Mathilde caught between two worlds as she wrestled with grief – saying a Christian prayer, smudging her face according to Wabanaki custom, and sorely discomforted by conflicting views on the afterlife of her child. For me, fleshing out such significant, yet undocumented, experiences in these women's lives by envisioning them in their own particular cultural realities, not only brought the women to life, but also shed light on their distinctive roles in history. I hope that it does the same for readers.

One thing seems clear. If we limit ourselves to documented records alone, the life histories of Native American women – especially those who lived prior to this century – will remain largely unwritten. Neither diplomats nor warriors, they were not on the cutting edge of tribal relations with those members of colonial society who kept written record of individuals and events. Rarely and barely noted, they remain hidden beyond the historical horizon. Yet it seems obvious that these women, as much as Native men, participated in the struggle for survival from generation to generation. They too made vital choices concerning adaptation and resistance in the face of colonial aggression. If we make no effort to research the stories of Native American women and incorporate them into the wider historical picture, our images of the past will remain incomplete and therefore inaccurate.

The reconstructions included in each story (and listed below) are integral to my attempt to help balance our understanding of the past. Readers can assume that all other scenes and quotes are recounted from reliable historical sources included in the reference list below. The passages that open each chapter are my own words.

MOLLY MATHILDE (CA. 1665–1717)

Some scholars believe that Molly and Mathilde are two distinct women – the first and second wives of the Baron of St. Castin. Others contend that both names belonged to one woman – the baron's sole wife. I have adopted the second view, put forth by Pierre Daviault and endorsed by Gorham Munson as "a plausible supposition." Since both views are debatable on strictly historical grounds, my decision ultimately rests on two additional factors. First, focusing on one woman brought a certain fluidity and intensity to the narrative. Second, and most important, Molly Dellis was firmly committed to the "one wife" theory. I believe her conviction sprang from her heart as well as from her head. In her own quest for love and emotional security, the one-wife theory grounded her, for she found comfort in contemplating a devoted and enduring seventeenth-century French-Indian couple whose cross-cultural union had survived the perils of epidemics, colonial warfare, and racial divisiveness. For example, in one letter to her own husband-to-be, Molly Dellis wrote the following: "Yes darling Johnny, Castin had but one Indian wife, to show the savages and his own people that God is not pleased with inconstant men. And before God, your wife remains Molly."

Reconstructions

As noted in the first "Portage" chapter, very few particular facts about Molly Mathilde's life entered the historical record. Typically, she is a shadow in the background in numerous accounts about her husband and, to a lesser degree, her father. Her story, in contrast to the other three women in this book, consists largely of reconstructed scenes placed in the context of actual historical events. Descriptions of her role in those events, and her responses to them, are based primarily on what we know in general about the lives of Wabanaki women of her day. They also draw from my understanding of the kind of questions Molly Dellis brought to her personal quest to bring this remote foremother's life to light.

References

The sources I consulted for Molly Mathilde's story are housed in the University of Maine Library in Orono and the Archives Departementales in Pau, France – except for Molly Dellis Nelson Archambaud's personal papers. The most essential references in the following list are Archambaud, Le Blant, Daviault, Godfrey, Faulkner and Faulkner, de Maluquer, Munson, and Wheeler.

Archambaud, Molly Dellis Nelson. 1935–1941. Personal papers. These include several letters between Molly Dellis and Jean Archambaud, touching on the subject of St. Castin and Molly Mathilde, plus eighteen pages of research notes on the subject (six of which are typed). Copies are in possession of the author and Molly Dellis's daughter, Jean Archambaud Moore.

Baker, Emerson et al., eds. 1992. *American Beginnings: Exploration, Culture and Cartography in the Land of Norumbega.* Lincoln: University of Nebraska Press.

Baxter, James Phinney, ed. 1889–1916. *Documentary History of the State of Maine, Containing the Baxter Manuscripts.* Vols. 5, 6, 10. Portland ME: The Thurston Print.

Churchill, Edwin A. 1995. The European Discovery of Maine and English Beachheads in Seventeenth-Century Maine. In *Maine: The*

Pine Tree State from Prehistory to the Present. Ed Richard Judd, et al. Orono: University of Maine Press.

Daviault, Pierre. 1939. *Le Baron de Saint-Castin, Chef Abenaquis.* Montreal: Editions de l'A.C.F.

Faulkner, Alaric, and Gretchen Faulkner. 1995. Acadian Settlement, 1607–1700. In *Maine: The Pine Tree State from Prehistory to the Present.* Ed. Richard Judd, et al. Orono: University of Maine Press.

————. 1987. *The French at Pentagoet, 1635–1674: An Archaeological Portrait of the Acadian Frontier.* Augusta: Maine Historic Preservation Commission. This book offers the most comprehensive look at seventeenth-century Pentagoet.

Ghere, David L. 1995. Diplomacy and War on the Maine Frontier, 1678–1759. In *Maine: The Pine Tree State from Prehistory to the Present.* Ed. Richard Judd, et al. Orono: University of Maine Press.

Godfrey, John E. 1876. Jean Vincent, Baron de Saint-Castin. In *Collections of the Maine Historical Society.* Vol. 7. Bath, England: E. Upton.

Le Blant, Robert. 1934. *Une Figure Légendaire de l'Histoire Acadienne: Le Baron de St-Castin.* Dax, France: Editions P. Pradeu. Le Blant's book includes period correspondence and other documents concerning St. Castin and his family estate in France.

Leger, Mary C. 1929. *The Catholic Indian Missions of Maine, 1611–1820.* Vol. 8. Washington DC: Catholic University of Washington, Studies in American Church History.

Le Grand Arrangement des Acadiens au Quebec: Notes de Petite Histoire Généalogies France, Acadie, Québec de 1625 à 1925. 1981. Montreal: Editions Elysée.

Longfellow, Henry Wadsworth. 1975. The Baron of St. Castine. In *The Poetical Works of Longfellow.* Ed. Horace E. Scudder. Boston: Houghton Mifflin Co.

Maluquer, Dufau de. 1895–96. *La Maison D'Abbadie de Maslacq.* Mémoires de la Société Royale du Canada, 1er série, vol. 1.

Manross, Brooke Ann. 1994. "The Freedom of Commerce": The History and Archaeology of Trade at St. Castin's Habitation 1670–1701. Master's thesis, University of Maine, Orono.

Morrison, Kenneth M. 1984. *The Embattled Northeast: The Elusive*

Ideal of Alliance in Abenaki-Euramerican Relations. Berkeley: University of California Press.

Munson, Gorham. 1965. St. Castin: A Legend Revised. *Dalhousie Review* 45, no. 3 (autumn): 338–60.

Prins, Harald E. L. 1996. *The Mi'kmaq: Resistance, Accommodation, and Cultural Survival.* New York: Harcourt Brace.

———. 1995. Turmoil on the Wabanaki Frontier, 1524–1678. In *Maine: The Pine Tree State from Prehistory to the Present.* Ed. R. Judd, et al. Orono: University of Maine Press.

———. 1994. The Children of Gluskap: Wabanaki Indians on the Eve of the European Invasion. In *American Beginnings: Exploration, Culture, and Cartography in the Land of Norumbega.* Ed. Emerson W. Baker, et al. Lincoln: University of Nebraska Press.

———. 1992. Cornfields at Meductic: Ethic and Territorial Reconfigurations in Colonial Acadia. *Man in the Northeast* 44 (fall): 1–18.

———. 1981–91. Wabanaki History Notebooks: Chronological and Thematic. Unpublished. In the possession of Harald Prins.

Prins, Harald E. L., and Bruce J. Bourque. 1987. Norridgewock: Village Translocation on the New England–Acadian Frontier. *Man in the Northeast* 33 (spring): 137–58.

Salagnac, Georges Cerbelaud. 1969. Abbadie de Saint-Castin. In *Dictionary of Canadian Biography.* Vol. 2 (1701–40). Toronto, Canada: University of Toronto Press.

Sprague, John Francis. 1915. *Baron de Saint Castin.* Portland ME: Smith and Sale, printers.

Sullivan, James. 1970. *History of the District of Maine.* Boston: I. Thomas and E. T. Andrews, 1795. Reprint, Augusta: Maine State Museum.

Thwaites, Reuben G., ed. 1959. *The Jesuit Relations and Allied Documents: Travels and Explorations of the Jesuit Missionaries in New France, 1710–1791.* 73 vols. Cleveland: Burrows, 1896–1901. Reprint, New York: Pageant, New York. Includes the original French, Latin, and Italian texts with English translations and notes.

Webster, John C. 1934. *Acadia at the End of the Seventeenth Century: Letters, Journals, and Memoirs of Joseph Robineau de Villebon, Commandant in Acadia, 1690–1700, and Other Contemporary Doc-*

uments. Monograph Series 1. St. John, Canada: New Brunswick Museum.

Wheeler, George A. 1896. *Castine Past and Present: The Ancient Settlement of Pentagoet and the Modern Town.* Boston: Rockwell and Churchill Press.

Wheeler, George A., and Louise Wheeler Bartlett. 1923. *History of Castine, Penobscot and Brooksville, Maine.* Cornwall NY: privately printed. Includes extensive official correspondence concerning Acadia, including Pentagoet, in St. Castin's period.

Williamson, William D. 1832. *History of Maine: From its First Discovery, A.D. 1602, to the Separation, A.D. 1820, Inclusive.* Hallowell ME: Glazier, Masters.

MOLLY OCKETT (CA. 1740–1816)

Unlike most women of her day, Indians and non-Indians alike, Molly Ockett caught the attention of people with pens. Typically, those who made note of her told about her experiences with white settlers. Some are first-hand accounts. Others are the result of interviews with people who knew her. They provide physical descriptions as well as specific stories about her. A few offer direct quotes from her, which are particularly helpful in shedding light on her character.

Reconstructions

The pages that describe the Pigwackets' exile in Massachusetts are based on volumes 21–24 of the *Journal of the House of Representatives of Massachusetts Bay*, 36 vols. (Boston: Massachusetts Historical Society, 1719–1764). Molly Ockett's subsequent stay as a servant girl with a Boston judge is conjecture, built on the same reference and the 1749 Treaty with the Eastern Indians at Falmouth cited in the *Maine Historical Society Collections at Falmouth*, 1st ser., 4:145–67.

The description of Molly Ockett as a teenager canoeing to an offshore island comes from my own experience kayaking the same waters we know she canoed.

The scene of Molly Ockett hiding behind a bush during the 1759 attack by Roger's Rangers on the French mission village at Odanak is built on the oral tradition of her survival, ultimately noted in writing by Nathaniel True (1863).

The description of Molly trying to read the minds of her white patients is conjecture, based on what is known of her personality as described by Barrows, Lapham, True (1863), Tufts, and Wilkens, among others.

The account of Molly Ockett seeking refuge in the woods where she communed with her foremothers is an effort on my part to imagine the thoughts of a self-possessed woman who refused to stay settled in one place. So are the thoughts attributed to her several pages later concerning "precious movement." See True (1874:12) and Lapham (178).

The description of Molly Ockett and her thoughts during her sojourn in Boston as an old woman comes from an account of her discomfort there. See Lapham (80).

The portrayal of Molly Ockett's final months living alone in a wigwam near Captain Bragg's home in East Andover is an elaboration of terse accounts by True (1863).

References

Much of what has been written about Molly Ockett is inaccurate. Reliable sources include the writings of nineteenth-century historian Nathaniel True, whose work was based on interviews of and correspondence with people who knew her. Although Henry Tufts was a shady character his personal narrative of his 1772–75 association with Molly Ockett and other Abenakis is valuable in that it provides a first-hand account of her life. Also of particular value are works by Lapham and Willey and Woodrow's book about Molly's friend Metallak. The latter profiles Molly and Sabattis, as well as Metallak, and includes a chapter on Abenaki chief Tomhegan's 1781 Bethel raid – a near-transcription of Lieutenant Segar's first-hand account of the raid and his captivity. All of the above resources, along with other accounts of Molly Ockett's life, can be found at the Bethel Historical Society. Some of this material is also available at the Maine State Library in Augusta and the Maine Historical Society in Portland. For a more conventional scholarly treatment of Molly Ockett's life, see Bunny McBride and Harald E. L. Prins (1996).

Barrows, John Stuart. 1938. *Fryeburg, Maine: An Historical Sketch.* Fryeburg ME.

Baxter, James Phinney, ed. 1889–1916. *Documentary History of the State of Maine, Containing the Baxter Manuscripts.* Vols. 10, 23, 24. Portland ME: The Thurston Print.

Beedy, Helen Coffin. 1895. Dusky Mothers. In *Mothers of Maine.* Portland ME: The Thurston Print.

Bennett, Randall H. 1991. *Bethel, Maine: An Illustrated History.* Bethel ME: Bethel Historical Society.

Butler, Joyce. 1995. Family and Community Life in Maine, 1783–1861. In *Maine: The Pine Tree State from Prehistory to the Present.* Ed. Richard Judd, et al. Orono: University of Maine Press.

Calloway, Colin. 1990. *The Western Abenakis of Vermont, 1600–1800.* Norman: University of Oklahoma Press.

Hamlin, Charles Eugene. 1899. *The Life and Times of Hannibal Hamlin.* Cambridge: Riverside Press.

Lapham, William B. 1981. *History of the Town of Bethel.* Facsimile of the 1891 edition, with a new historical essay by Stanley Russell Howe. Bethel ME: New England History Press and Bethel Historical Society.

McBride, Bunny, and Harald E. L. Prins. 1996. Walking the Medicine Line: Molly Ockett, a Pigwacket Doctor. In *Northeastern Indian Lives, 1632–1816.* Ed. Robert Grumet. Amherst: University of Massachusetts Press.

Morrison, Kenneth M. 1984. *The Embattled Northeast: The Elusive Ideal of Alliance in Abenaki-Euramerican Relations.* Berkeley: University of California Press.

Newell, Catherine S. C. 1981. *Molly Ockett.* Bethel ME: Bethel Historical Society.

Prins, Harald E. L. 1996. *The Mi'kmaq: Resistance, Accommodation, and Cultural Survival.* New York: Harcourt Brace.

———. 1981–91. Wabanaki History Notebooks: Chronological and Thematic. Unpublished. In the possession of Harald Prins.

Rivard, Paul. 1990. *Maine Sawmills: A History.* Augusta: Maine State Museum.

True, Nathaniel T. 1874. Historical Address. Report of the Centennial Celebration at Bethel, 26 Aug. Portland ME: B. Thurston.

————. 1867. The Parallel between Barbarism and Civilization. *Oxford Democrat*, 12 July.

————. 1863. The Last of the Pequakets: Molly-Ockett. *Oxford (ME) Democrat*, 2 Jan. Reprint, Bethel Historical Society Newsletter 2, no. 2 (June 1978).

————. 1859–61. History of Bethel. *Bethel (ME) Courier*.

Tufts, Henry. 1807. *Narrative of the Life, Adventures, Travels, and Sufferings of Henry Tufts, Now Residing at Lemington, in the District of Maine, in Substance, as Compiled from his Own Mouth.* Dover NH: Samuel Bragg Jr. Reprinted as *The Autobiography of a Criminal: Henry Tufts.* Ed. Edmund Pearson. New York: Duffield, 1930.

Wilkins, Martha Fifield. 1977. *Sunday River Sketches: A New England Chronicle.* Ed. Randy Bennett. Rumford ME: Androscoggin.

Willey, Benjamin. 1869. *History of the White Mountains.* Boston: N.p.

————. 1856. *Incidents of White Mountain History.* Boston: Nathaniel Noyes.

Winthrop, John Sr. 1853. *The History of New England from 1630 to 1649. From His Original Manuscripts.* Ed. James Savage. 2 vols. Boston: Little, Brown.

Woodrow, Arthur. 1928. *Story of Metallak: Last of the Cooashaukes.* Rumford ME: Rumford Publishing.

MOLLY MOLASSES (CA. 1775–1867)

Even though information about Molly Molasses is scarce, some reliable sources include a few descriptions of direct encounters with her and even a few quotes. Much of her enigmatic life history was pieced together by tracing the life of John Neptune, who fathered her four children.

Reconstructions

The idea that in 1816 Molly Molasses tried to rally support for Neptune among women is a supposition, based on her well-established affinity with him, the legendary power of her personality, and numerous historical references to the keen interest Penobscot women had in *boodawazin* (talking politics).

The depiction of Molly Molasses doing the honor dance at Neptune's and Attean's inauguration comes from the assumption that she was among dancers described in an eye-witness account of that event. The account is reprinted in Dillingham.

The statement that Molly Molasses "passed some time" with Neptune during his self-imposed exile at Moxie Pond is conjecture, based on reports that it was one of the places where she camped. There is no specific evidence that she camped there during that time.

That Molly Molasses was baffled by the vast stretches of forest being "off limits" to Indians is surmise, as is her son's tale of being accused of poaching and the scene of a farmer chasing her and her daughter off his land when they were looking for basket ash. While there is no specific evidence that Molly and her children experienced these things, they were common occurrences among Penobscots at the time and could well have happened to them.

The representation of Penobscots being on edge in the face of mounting change and turmoil – to the point that tempers flared and voices turned shrill – is an effort to capture the emotional impact that the documented historical changes must have had on the group.

The images of Molly Molasses in Brewer, hiking through the woods to town in order to trade with Hardy and others builds on Eckstorm's account of Molly (1945), which includes a description of her notorious bargaining skills. The thoughts attributed to Molly in this section are speculations, based on the dilemmas she faced concerning her relationship with Hardy and pressures to acculturate. The scene of her looking in the mirror at the general store is imagined, although the description of the store is drawn from historical accounts.

Molly Molasses looking at posters in front of the Bangor Theater is based on newspaper theater ads of the day, coupled with the knowledge that she was often in Bangor.

Molly Molasses's "rules" about give and take, described after the true stolen moose-hide incident, are surmised, based on her behavior and written records stating that old-time Penobscots did not tolerate theft. Eckstorm (1945) notes Molly's honesty. Jonathan Hardy's son, Manly, quoted in "Old Molly Molasses," describes Molly as "strictly honest."

The final scene of Molly Molasses walking along the river in Bangor during a snowstorm is imagined, as are her thoughts. They, like the opening paragraph of the chapter, are rooted in various first-person accounts of Molly in her old age – all of them portraying her as a tough and intimidating woman. For example, see Eckstorm (1945), "Molly Molasses," "Old Molly Molasses," and Swartz.

References

The following sources are located primarily in the Bangor Historical Society and The University of Maine Library, Orono. Eckstorm's work offers by far the most complete account of Molly Molasses and her consort John Neptune. Norton's book and various Penobscot Indian agent reports, along with the writing of Allin and Judd, Eastman, Prins, and Rivard, provided helpful historical context.

Allin, Lawrence C., and Richard W. Judd. 1995. Creating Maine's Resource Economy, 1783–1861. In *Maine: The Pine Tree State from Prehistory to the Present*. Ed. Richard Judd, et al. Orono: University of Maine Press.

Barker, David. 1876. *Poems by David Barker, with Biographical Sketch by Hon. John E. Godfrey*. 3d ed. Bangor ME: Lewis Barker. Among these poems is "To Moll Molasses," 222–23.

The Centennial Celebration of the Settlement of Bangor, 1870. Bangor ME: Town Committee of Arrangements.

Dillingham, Charles. Ca. 1900. *The Penobscot*. Bangor ME: N.p. This thirty-six-page booklet includes a portrait and brief profile of Molly Molasses, as well as a drawing of John Neptune and an eye-witness account of his inauguration.

Dillingham, George F. 1868. Penobscot Agent's Report. In *Annual Report of the Agents of The Penobscot and Passamaquoddy Tribes of Indians and of the Supervisors of the Schools for Indians at Old Town and Pleasant Point, 1867*.

———. 1865. *Reports of the Indian Agent and Superintendent on Farming of the Penobscot Tribe of Indians 1864*. Augusta: State of Maine.

Eastman, Joel W., and Paul E. Rivard. 1995. Transportation and Manufacturing. In *Maine: The Pine Tree State from Prehistory to the Present.* Ed. Richard Judd, et al. Orono: University of Maine Press.

Eckstorm, Fannie Hardy. 1945. *Old John Neptune and Other Maine Indian Shamans.* Portland ME: The Southworth-Anthoenson Press. This book includes a short profile of Molly Molasses, 16–25.

———. 1941. *Indian Place Names of the Penobscot Valley and the Maine Coast.* Orono: University of Maine Press.

Foster, Charles H., ed. 1975. *Down East Diary by Benjamin Browne Foster.* Orono: University of Maine Press. Written between 1847 and 1853, this diary offers a look at Orono and Bangor in Molly Molasses's day.

Godfrey, John Edwards. 1979. *The Journals of John Edwards Godfrey.* Rockland ME: Courier-Gazette. The writer tells of encounters with Molly Molasses, 230–33, 312.

Hubbard, John. 1852. *Report of the Indian Agent to the Thirty-First Legislature* [S. No. 45.] Augusta: State of Maine. 3 March 1851. File no. I32/2.1:1851. This is a narrative report on the Penobscot and Passamaquoddy tribes, coupled with 1847–51 financial overview by the Indian agents.

Molly Molasses, *The Jeffersonian,* 14 January 1868. This short article recounts the story of Molly helping herself to a pile of dropped potatoes on the wharf in Belfast, Maine, and her ability to elicit free passage on all river steamers.

Norton, David. 1881. *Sketches of the Town of Old Town, Penobscot County, Maine, from Its Earliest Settlement to 1879; with Biographical Sketches.* Bangor ME: S. G. Robinson.

Old Molly Molasses. *Bangor (ME) Daily Whig and Courier.* No date. Photocopy of article in author's possession.

Prins, Harald E. L. 1998. Chief Big Thunder (1827–1906): The Life History of a Penobscot Trickster. *Maine History* 37, no. 3 (winter 1998): 140–58.

———. 1981–91. Wabanaki Notebooks: Chronological and Thematic. Unpublished. In the possession of Harald Prins.

Purinton, James A. 1861. Penobscot Indians. In *Reports of the Indian Agents of the State of Maine 1861.* Augusta: State of Maine.

———. 1860. Penobscot Indians. In *Reports of the Indian Agents of the State of Maine 1860.* Augusta: State of Maine.

Sawyer, Candace Loud, and Laura Loud Orcutt. 1979. *The Journals of John Edwards Godfrey*. Rockland ME: Courier-Gazette.

Stephenson, Isaac. 1915. *Recollections of a Long Life, 1829–1915*. Chicago: N.p.

Swartz, Brian. 1990. Indian Women Made Influence Felt. *Bangor (ME) Daily News*, March 3–4.

Thayer, Mildred N., and Mrs. Edward W. Ames. 1962. The Indians in Brewer. In *Brewer, Orrington, Holden, Eddington: History and Families*. Brewer ME: 150th Anniversary Committee.

Thoreau, Henry David. 1966. *The Maine Woods*. New York: Thomas Crowell.

Wheeler, George A., and H. W. Wheeler. 1878. *History of Brunswick, Topsham, and Harpswell Maine, Including the Ancient Territory Known as Pejepscot*. Boston: Alfred Mudge.

Whitten, Jean Patten. 1975. Fanny Hardy Eckstorm: A Descriptive Bibliography. *Northeast Folklore*. Vol. 16. Orono: Northeast Folklore Society, Northeast Archives of Folklore and Oral History, Department of Anthropology, University of Maine, Orono.

MOLLY DELLIS NELSON ARCHAMBAUD (1903–1977)

This profile draws from my full-length biography, *Molly Spotted Elk: A Penobscot in Paris* (Norman: University of Oklahoma Press, 1995), which provides detailed notes and an exhaustive bibliography of primary and secondary sources, including Molly Dellis's diaries and her other personal papers. See also my essay, "The Spider and the WASP: Chronicling the Life of Molly Spotted Elk," in *Reading Beyond Words: Contexts for Native History*, edited by Jennifer S. H. Brown and Elizabeth Vibert (Peterborough, Canada: Broadview Press, 1996), 403–28.

Reconstructions

Given the wealth of information available about Molly Dellis, reconstructions are few and were used primarily to strengthen the telling of her story and the portage chapters.

The book's opening scene in the first portage is an imagined re-creation based on the fact that Molly Dellis researched the life of Molly Mathilde in the New York Public Library. In contrast, the second, third, and fourth portages each contain a fictionalized narrative device: Molly Dellis's decision to research and write about the lives of Molly Ockett, Molly Molasses, and herself. Other than this, these portage chapters follow the facts of Molly Dellis's life.

The scene of Molly Dellis's encounter with Hemlock Joe and Frank Speck in the first pages of her own profile is rooted in her frequent references to Hemlock Joe, including an unpublished personal narrative she wrote in 1938 in which she told of "earning stories" by doing chores. It is not certain that she and Speck were ever with Joe at the same time, but it is likely that they were (see McBride 1995, 30–32).

At some point, Molly Dellis told Jean Archambaud the story of Molly Mathilde and St. Castin for the first time. In all likelihood this occurred during their first hike in the Pyrenees Mountains. I have re-created this first telling based on Molly Dellis's diaries and my own 1998 visit to the region.

The description of Molly Dellis's vision (or dream) of the other three Mollies is based on several facts: she loved spending time by the river; she dreamed often and always took great note of her dreams; and she sought answers to her questions about life in nature and in the history of her ancestors.

The scene in which two young Penobscot women come to Molly Dellis for cultural insights builds upon comments from several Penobscots from a younger generation who have told me that they visited her to learn about the past, including the old legends.

Molly Dellis's springtime encounter with the woodcock is under-girded by her love for and knowledge of nature; the presence of this bird along the Penobscot River; and the clear indications in her diary that her joy came from her love of dance, family, and tradition.

The scene in the final portage comes from the fact that Molly Dellis often looked to the moon and thought of her husband whom she nicknamed Neebowset (Night Walker), the Penobscot word for moon. And she did, indeed, die falling down the back stairs leading to the kitchen.

ILLUSTRATIONS

The images used to illustrate Molly Molasses's and Molly Dellis's stories are actual photographs of these women. Although Molly Mathilde and Molly Ockett were also authentic historical figures, there are no known images of them. In fact, I am not aware of a single picture of a Penobscot or Pigwacket woman made during the time that the two women lived. We can, however, gain a sense of how they looked through paintings made of Mi'kmaq women who lived during the same period. According to colonial records of their day, in terms of dress and general appearance, it was often impossible to distinguish one Wabanaki tribe from another. In large part this was owing to widespread intermarriage among the tribes.

PORTAGE IMAGE. Detail from Jean-Baptiste Louis Franquelin's "Carte pour servir à l'éclaircissement du Papier Terrier de la Nouvelle-France." 1678. NMC 17393 / From a copy at the National Archives of Canada. Original held at the Bibliothèque Nationale, Paris, France, S.H.Pf. 125, div. 1, no. 1. By permission of the National Archives of Canada.

CHAPTER 1. Detail from a watercolor that pictures an Abenaki woman and man from one of the French mission villages on the St. Lawrence River. Ca. 1750. Artist unknown. Gagnon Collection, City of Montreal Records Management and Archives. By permission of the City of Montreal Records Management and Archives.

CHAPTER 2. Detail from "Micmac Encampment Near Halifax, Nova Scotia." 1791. Watercolor by Hibbert Newton Binney. From the history collection of the Nova Scotia Museum, Halifax. By permission of the Nova Scotia Museum.

CHAPTER 3. Photograph of Molly Molasses. Ca. 1865. Collections of the Bangor Historical Society. Photo no. 106. By permission of the Bangor Historical Society.

CHAPTER 4. Photograph of Molly Dellis. Ca. 1930. By permission of Jean Archambaud Moore.